ABORTIONS

IN THE CHURCH

WORKBOOK

ABORTIONS

IN THE CHURCH

Divine Strategies to
Spiritual Deliverance

WORKBOOK

Author Derashay Zorn

For information about special discounts for bulk purchase, contact the sales department at **sales@inthechurch.com**

Designed by D' Technology

D.O.R.M. International Publishing
Visit our website at **www.divine-order.org**
Printed in the United State of America
First Edition: February 2017
10 9 8 7 6 5 4 3 2 1
Library of Congress Cataloging-in-Publication Data
Derashay Worthen-Zorn
Abortions in The Church-Divine Strategies to Spiritual Deliverance/ Derashay Worthen-Zorn – 1st ed.
ISBN-13: 978-0986249310
ISBN-10: 0986249319

Table of Contents

Introduction

Instructions: Read these instructions before examining and diagnosing any patient.

This workbook is designed to help sharpen, prove, and grow your knowledge and understanding of spiritual influences that are causing individuals to have a spiritual miscarriage, abortion, or stillborn with their goals, dreams, visions, desires, and purpose. It is a companion tool resource to the Abortion "In The Church" Divine Strategies to Spiritual Deliverance book to equip the body of Christ in delivering the word of God for their life. This book is a medical guide to assist and train individuals in, assessing, diagnosing and overcoming hindrances that cause individuals to have a spiritual miscarriage, abortion, or stillborn with their promises and purpose from God.

This workbook will train and equip individuals understanding of spiritual miscarriages, abortions, and stillbirths with hands on experience through studying different individuals in the bible at various aspects in their walk with God. It includes, 21 Biblical patient case studies for individuals to examine and diagnose a certain aspect in the patient lives to determine if they are having a spiritual miscarriage, abortion, or stillborn. In addition, to provide them with medical advice to avoid having a spiritual miscarriage, abortion, or stillborn with Gods word.

It contains a mixture of activities and guidance which combines principles learned from the Abortion "In The Church" Divine Strategies to Spiritual Deliverance book.

Use the activities and guidance to create or collect evidence and to chart your professional diagnoses of your patient.

PURPOSE OF THIS WORKBOOK

This workbook has three main objectives

1. To provide a foundation of biblical knowledge and understanding on spiritual influences that are causing individuals to have spiritual miscarriages, abortions, or stillborn with their goals, dreams, desires, visions, and purpose.
2. To give you practice in examining and diagnosing patient's situation to expose areas in their past and present that is causing their goals, dreams, desires, visions, and purpose to die.
3. To train you in analyzing situations to diagnose and provide solutions to help avoid spiritual miscarriages, abortions, or stillbirths through the utilization of biblical principles.

SYSTEM OF BIBLE REFERENCES

The translation of the Bible used throughout this course is New International Version and the English Standard Version. The working in your version may be slightly different. However, the truths trained in this course are cohesive in any reliable version.

HOW TO USE THE WORKBOOK

At the start of each patient chart, you will find the name of your patient and the scripture study reference for them. You are to read and examine the study Scripture before attempting to diagnose any patient. You are also free to read or study any information concerning your patient before your current scripture study to obtain background information on your patient. This information will help you in appropriately examine and diagnosing your client current state per the study scripture.

These sections are to help you sharpen your discernment in identifying different spirits that are causing your patient from giving birth to the word of God. In addition to being able to apply the same tool in helping yourself and other around avoiding having a spiritual miscarriage, abortion, or stillborn.

The patient chart, of activities and information in this workbook, are broken down as follows:

Patient Name: Each chart starts with a patient name so that you can identify which patient you are diagnosing in the test.

Scripture Study: This section is used to obtain the scripture references to diagnose your patient current condition. Find and read your patient situation in your Bible. Evaluate and diagnose your patient behavior in the text. Chart your patient behavior under immunization or infections, diseases, and allergies section.

Vital Statistics: The vital statistics section will provide important background information on the patient such as living location, career information, family lineage, and social groups.

Immunizations: The immunization area is used to identify godly characteristics in your patient that could be conducive to their situation. You can identify character traits for your patient past and present from other areas of the Bible. (if you chose) However, it must consist of instances that took place before your scripture study text. The character traits listed here can go beyond your study scripture. Along with finding the trait, you are to provide an example being exemplified, in them. This information can be used to help you build your patient physical history and confidential notes. *Immunizations* are defined as godly character traits that are identified, in your patient past or present behavior.

Infections/Diseases/ Allergies: This section is used to identify character traits in your patient that could influence them in having a spiritual miscarriage, abortion, or stillborn. You can identify character traits for your patient past and present from other areas of the Bible. (if you chose) However, it must consist of instances that took place before your scripture study text. Along with finding the trait, you are to provide an example being exemplified, in them. The infection, diseases, and allergies identified can be used as an aid for your patient, physical history and confidential notes. *Infections, diseases, and allergies* are defined as ungodly character traits that can be identified, within your patient past or present behavior.

Physical History: The physical history section is used to provide a synopsis of the patient past medical history. It identifies anything that has taken place in their lives up until the point of the

study scripture. These notes are vital so that other physicians can quickly review the medical history of the patient to aid them in their current doctor visit.

Lab work: Ordered Test: The Lab work/order test area is based upon the individual assignment according to the study Scripture or assignment that led up to the study scripture. You may come across patients, who you will not find a direct assignment on and you will have to use context clues to identify, their assignment. For example, Sarai was the wife of Abram and because his assignment was to be the father of many nations. By default, her assignment is to become the mother of many nations and bear him a son. Cain, to bring God an acceptable offering. Hannah, to receive the love of her husband unconditionally.

Confidential Patient Notes: The confidential patient notes section is used to diagnose the current condition of the patient based upon the study Scripture. It should also indicate the patient final diagnostic condition. These notes should be written last as all other components will help build and support this section of the patient notes.

Lab Work Results: The Lab work results section should identify the outcome or possible outcome of the study scripture.

Prenatal Diagnoses This section is used to help aid in your patient diagnoses for treatment according to the scripture study.

Prenatal Aftercare Treatment: This section is used to provide medical advice or a treatment plan for your client or future patient to assist them in avoiding having a spiritual miscarriage, abortion, or stillborn with their dreams, goals, purpose, aspirations, vision, etc.

Prescription Scripture(s): This section is used to prescribe your patient with scriptures that they can use to help them avoid having a spiritual miscarriage, abortion, or stillborn.

Reflections: This section is used to identify with your personal life and its correlation to an area in the patient's life.

Workbook Answers: Go to www.inthechurch.com/abortions

Spiritual Miscarriage

Every thought that God put in the heart of man has the potential to bring forth light into dark places for the edification of other to be perfection in the body of Christ.

The loss is in the seed that never had the opportunity to give life

When anyone hears the message about the kingdom and does not understand it, the evil one comes and snatches away what was sown in his heart. This is the seed sown along the path. *Matthew 13:19 (NIV)*

Patient Chart
Sarai / Sarah

Scripture Study: Genesis [DZ1]**16**

Vital Statistics

- **Location Lived:** Ur of the Chaldees, Babylonia, then moved with him to Canaan
- **Career:** Wife, mother, household manager
- **Family:** Father: Terah. Husband: Abraham. Half brothers: Nahor and Haran. Nephew: Lot. Son: Isaac.
- **Social group:** Abimelech, Melchizedek

Immunizations:

- **Loyalty:** Was intensely loyal to Abram
- **Self-Sacrificial:** She sacrificed herself for her husband sake
- **Love:** She had great love for Abram
- **Support:** She upheld every move Abram made
- **Faith:** She followed her husband in God word for his life

Infections/Diseases/ Allergies:

- **Unfruitful/Barren:** Sarai womb was barren and she was unable to conceive
- **Doubt:** She had trouble believing God's promises to her
- **Impatience:** Sarai took matters into her own hands instead of waiting on God
- **Self-Reliance:** She planned her own solution to bring forth the promise of God for their lives. Sarai did not consult God with her plans
- **Anger:** She treated Hagar harshly.
- **Blame:** Said the Lord had closed her womb & Abram was the reason Hagar despised her.
- **Jealousy:** Resentful over Hagar conception and relationship between Abram and Hagar
- **Carnality:** She adapted to the customs of their society.
- **Seductive:** Did not conceal her beauty instead exposed herself unto the men of the land
- **Shame:** Sarai was public rebuked for lying to King Pharaoh. She had not been able to conceive a child
- **Embarrassed:** Got evicted out of Egypt for lying to King Pharaoh. The talk of the town
- **Liar:** Told King Pharaoh and princes of the land that she was Abraham sister
- **Adulteress:** When into Pharaohs palace
- **Worthlessness:** Went along with things that would degrade her

Physical History:

Sarai is the wife of Abram from Chaldees. She was loyal to him and wanted the best for his life. Sarai left her family behind to follow Abram in what God had put in his heart. Her love and trust in him, were great as she sacrificed herself on many occasions for his sake. Sarai desired to have a child by Abram and in spite of all her sacrificing she had no control over her capacity to conceive. This effect Sarai self-esteem about herself. As she was known to flaunt, her beauty around even when it would put herself and husband in danger. Sarai found herself facing starvation, adultery, eviction, shame, etc. due to her husband and her not trusting and believing in God.

During her time, it was a disgrace and a dishonor for any women who were barren. She was up in age and reaching a place where childbearing would be impossible when her husband Abram received the promise from God that his heir would come from himself. Genesis 15:4. Sarai has some great qualities in her and if she would apply them to her relationship, with God, they will cause her to excel beyond her imagination.

Lab work: Ordered Test:

- **Produce**: Bear a child for Abraham
- **Nurture**: Become the mother of nations

Confidential Patient Notes:

Sarai having the love of her life could not provide for him the one thing that society considered to make her worthy of him. She wanted to conceive a child desperately to prove her worth. As time passed, Sarai begins to look at her situation and struggled with its possibilities. Between her desire and God promise to Abram, her mind started to wonder, how could she become pregnant with a barren womb. She wrestles with the thought that God had shut up her womb and therefore, it was impossible for her to conceive a child for Abram. Her thoughts lead her to consider that she was not the one who God would give birth to Abram heir. Some problem arose in Sarah's reasoning because God would never compromise His word. The enemy begins to torment Sarai with her physical status and the spirit of hopelessness and destitute settled within.

This impossible situation made Sarai became impatient. Frustrated with the matter, she resulted to worldly reasoning. Sari devised a plan to help God fulfill his promise to Abram. She decides to give her maid servant Hagar to her husband. This decision caused chaos to break out in their home. Hagar became pregnant, by Abram and it caused more troubled Sarai. After conceiving her servant disliked her and began to disrespectful. I'm sure Hagar attention from Abram increase since she was pregnant with his first offspring. In his eyes, she was carrying the manifestation of God's promise unto him. The agony of seeing Hagar pregnant with Abram's child and receiving his attention stirred up anger, jealousy, frustration, bitterness, etc. toward her servant. Sarai blamed Abram for her suffering and started lashing out at Hagar. The environment became so unbearable from Sarai's harness that her servant ran away. Here, Abram and Sarai are faced with unnecessary drama because her impatience caused her to have a spiritual miscarriage with the word of God.

Lab Work Results:

- **Unproductive**: It did not bring forth the promise of God.
- **Chaos**: Caused tension In relationships
- **Trauma:** Caused and/or opened emotional wounds in Sarah and Hagar
- **Broken relationships:** negatively affected Sarai relationship with Hagar and Abram
- **Dependency:** Equipping Sarai to depend on him
- **Patience**: Teaching Sarah to leave matters in God's hand because of the warfare that her impatience has caused
- **Faith:** Training Sarah to have faith in God and turn to him in time of need

Prenatal Diagnoses

1. Can your patient be considered as a spiritual miscarriage patient? ❑ Yes ❑No

2. Explain your diagnoses.

   _____
   _____
   _____
   _____
   _____
   _____
   _____

3. Does your patient have any signs that could put them at high-risk of having a spiritual miscarriage? ❑ Yes ❑No

4. If so, chart the signs you have identified.

   ❑ Spiritual Maturity   ❑ Spiritual Dysfunctions   ❑ Paternal Traits
   ❑ Spiritual Trauma and Infections   ❑ Medications   ❑ Spiritual Diet
   ❑History of Spiritual Miscarriages ❑ Toxin Environment   ❑_____

5. Provide an explanation of your patient warning signs.

   _____
   _____
   _____
   _____
   _____
   _____
   _____

6. Is your patient having a spiritual miscarriage? ❑ Yes ❑No

7. If so, what sign(s) assisted you with your patient analyzes?
   ❑ Spiritual Ignorance   ❑Spiritual Bleeding   ❑Spiritual Torment

8. Chart the areas of infections that could lead to a spiritual miscarriage for your patient.

   _____   _____   _____
   _____   _____   _____
   _____   _____   _____

Prenatal Aftercare Treatment

Provide your patient with medical advice after care that would assist them from having a spiritual miscarriage.

_____
_____
_____
_____
_____
_____
_____

Prescription Scripture (s)

_____
_____
_____
_____
_____
_____

Reflections:

Have you ever decided to help God out because you were impatient and chaos broke loose? ❑ Yes ❑No

How did that decision effect you? Did it cause you more harm than good? How did it make you feel afterward? Was it worth it?

_____
_____
_____
_____
_____
_____

What lessons can you take away from Sarai to apply in your own life or situation?

_____
_____
_____
_____
_____
_____
_____

```
┌─────────────────────────────────┐
│          Patient Chart          │
│           Jeroboam              │
└─────────────────────────────────┘
```

Scripture Study: 1 Kings 12:20-14:20.

Vital Statistics:

- **Location Lived:** The northern kingdom of Israel
- **Careers**: Project foreman, king of Israel
- **Family:** Father: Nebat. Mother: Zeruah. Sons: Abijah, Nadab.
- **Social group:** Solomon, Nathan, Ahijah, Rehoboam

Immunizations:

- **Charismatic**: The people called for him and appointed him as king
- **Courage**: A mighty man of Valor
- **Diligent**: Solomon seen he was industrious
- **Effective Leader**: Solomon made he officer of the labor force
- **Organizer**: Supervised the labor for of the house of Joseph

Infections/Diseases/ Allergies:

- **Rebellion:** Rebelled against Solomon
- **Fear**: Thought that he, would be killed if the people went back and sacrificed at Jerusalem.
- **Insecure**: In spite of the people making him king, he thought that they would leave him and go back to the house of David.
- **Idolatry**: Erected idols in Israel to keep people away from the Temple in Jerusalem
- **Self-Reliance**: did not depend on God.
- **False Religion**: setup his own appointed festival, sacrificed to idols and appointed people outside of the priesthood to serve as priests in the temple.
- **Disobedient**: Did not follow the commands of God
- **Lack of Trust**: Did not trust God word.
- **Sedition**: Build altars and high places so that the people would not go to Jerusalem and worship so that they would turn back to the house of David.
- **Lack of Wisdom**: Listen to unwise advice to build idols.

Physical History:

Jeroboam was a man who had good leadership skills that were recognized by King Solomon and God. When King Solomon attitude changed toward God as a consequence, God took 10 of the tribes of Israel out of his hands. The person who God had chosen to take this prestige position was Jeroboam. He became the 1st King to rule over the ten tribes of Israel. God gave him the following commands: *"And if you will listen to all that I command you, and will walk in my ways, and do what is right in my eyes by keeping my statutes and my commandments, as David my servant did, I will be with you and will build you a sure house, as I built for David, and I will give Israel to you. **1 Kings 11:38 (ESV)".*** At that time, Jeroboam was not able to obtain the kingdom because he had to wait until King Solomon death. After the king's death and the right conditions, Jeroboam was handed the ten tribes as promised by God. After receiving the prophecy from Ahijah, He found himself fleeing for his life as King Solomon sought to kill him. Leaving everything behind, Jeroboam found himself hidden in Egypt to preserve his life.

Finally, King Solomon dies, and the tribal leaders call for Jeroboam. As he, arrives back in the city the leader chose him to speak on their behalf to Rehoboam. Jeroboam stood as the spokesperson for Israel to negotiate justice. However, Rehoboam took unwise advice and caused Israel to revolt. This opens the door for the prophecy from God to be fulfilled, in Jeroboam life. Israel leaders call and crown Jeroboam king over the ten tribes of Israel.

Lab work: Ordered Test:

- **Leadership**: To rule over the 10 northern tribes of Israel
- **Obedience**: Follow God's command,
- **Submission**: Walk in God's ways,
- **Faithful**: Do right in the eyes of God by keeping His statutes and commands,
- **Exemplify**: Follow the pattern of King David

Confidential Patient Notes:

The appointed time has arrived and Jeroboam is established as the king of Israel. Quickly, the newly established King went to work to fortify his kingdom. Strategically, he established his capital in Shechem and built up Penuel to take control over the entry and exit of his kingdom. Working hard to get everything in order he begins to wrestle with some things that would turn his heart from God. King Jeroboam received some negative thoughts and fear grip the heart of the king. He began to ponder on the possibilities of the kingdom returning unto the house of David. This thought tormented him and drove him to omit the word of God. Searching for the answer and the way to go Jeroboam found himself seeking advice that submitted to his thoughts. His counsel was very unwise and they could not have known the commandments of the Lord or the history of Israel. Because their actions lead them to repeat Israel history and breaking the Ten Commandments.

Jeroboam did not delay in the advice of his unwise counsel. Immediately, he erected idols, established a new form of religion, built false worship center, and installing high priest from outside of the tribe of the Levi. God sent a prophet to speak against the altar and king, but Jeroboam still gives a death ear. He did not repent and turn from his evil ways. Jeroboam had a great opportunity to do mighty things in his kingship. He allowed fear to take over and made decisions that would alter his life, family, and kingdom forever. It was a time, to turn to God for instruction but he never took the opportunity. This fear caused the king to do the opposite of what the Lord had instructed him to do. Therefore, it caused him to have a spiritual miscarriage that leads to the following consequences: reference: *1 Kings 14:10-16*

Lab Work Results:

- **Harden heart:** Would not turn from evil ways
- **Destruction**: Jeroboam kingdom would be destroyed
- **Premature Death**: Dishonorable death to every male (free or slave) under Jeroboam. Except for the sick son.
- **Burden**: The wife had to carry the burden of the sad news
- **Adversaries**: The Lord would raise up king to kill Jeroboam entire family.
- **Exile**: The entire nation of Israel would be struck down, uprooted, scattered, and sent into exile because they followed Jeroboam leadership and participated in false worship and idolatry.
- **Unprotected**: The removal of God's hands upon Israel because they followed his sin.

Prenatal Diagnoses

1. Was your patient a likely candidate for a spiritual miscarriage? ❑ Yes ❑No

2. Can your patient be diagnosed with any high-risk factor(s) that can potentially make them a candidate for a spiritual miscarriage?

   ❑ Spiritual Maturity   ❑ Spiritual Dysfunctions   ❑ Paternal Traits
   ❑ Spiritual Trauma and Infections   ❑ Medications   ❑ Spiritual Diet
   ❑History of Spiritual Miscarriages   ❑ Toxin Environment   ❑_____

3. If, so can you explain your diagnoses

   _____
   _____
   _____

4. Based upon your patient chart can you identify signs of a potential spiritual miscarriage?

   ❑ Yes ❑No

5. If so, what was the signs?

   ❑ Spiritual Ignorance   ❑Spiritual Bleeding   ❑Spiritual Torment

6. Chart the areas of infections that are warning signs for Jeroboam's spiritual miscarriage

   _____   _____   _____
   _____   _____   _____
   _____   _____   _____

Chart the diagnoses of your patient spiritual miscarriage.

_____
_____
_____

Prenatal Aftercare Treatment

Can you provide medical advice that would assist someone else that are having the same symptoms as your patient from having a spiritual miscarriage?

_____
_____
_____
_____
_____
_____
_____
_____

Prescription Scripture (s)

_____
_____
_____
_____
_____
_____
_____
_____

Reflections:

Have you ever been so afraid of losing friends that you compromised Gods word for your life?
❑ Yes No ❑

If so, what lead you to compromise? How did it make you feel afterward? Was it worth it?

_____
_____
_____
_____
_____
_____
_____

What lessons can you take away from Jeroboam to apply in your own life or situation?

_____
_____
_____
_____
_____
_____
_____

Patient Chart
Joseph

Scripture Study: Matthew 1:18-19

Vital Statistics

- **Location Lived:** Nazareth, Bethlehem
- **Career:** Carpenter
- **Family:** Wife: Mary. Children: Jesus, James, Joseph, Judas, Simon, and daughters
- **Social group:** Herod the Great, Simeon, Anna

Immunizations:

- **Integrity:** A man of integrity
- **Love:** Didn't want to expose marry
- **Patient:** Wait on answer from God
- **Trusted God:** A person sensitive to God's guidance and willing to do God's will no matter what the consequence
- **Prayer:** He went and prayed before he reacted on his emotions
- **Obedience:** He obeyed the Angels instructions

Infections/Diseases/ Allergies:

- **Anxiety:** He was going to divorce marry quietly
- **Disappointment:** He felt deceived by Mary being pregnant

Physical History:

Joseph an honorable man found himself in the middle of a God appointed assignment and social pressure as He found out his fiancé was pregnant. His fiancé was pledged, to him as a virgin and before the consummation of marriage, she reveals to him that she's pregnant by the Holy Spirit. Joseph just not comprehending Mary being pregnant without sleeping with a man decides he must divorce her quietly. His emotions of disappointment, betrayal, and disbelief lead him to this reasonable decision. Because of his great love for Mary, he didn't want her to become a public disgrace. As it wouldn't be long before, it was the talk of the town. He goes to sleep and is met by an Angel in his dream on the matter.

Lab work: Ordered Test:

- **Covenant:** Marry Mary

Confidential Patient Notes:

_____
_____
_____
_____
_____
_____
_____
_____
_____
_____
_____
_____
_____
_____
_____
_____
_____
_____
_____
_____
_____
_____
_____
_____
_____

Lab Work Results:

- _____
  _____
- _____
  _____
- _____
  _____
- _____
  _____

Prenatal Diagnoses

1. Was your patient a likely candidate for a spiritual miscarriage? ❑ Yes ❑No

2. Can your patient be diagnosed with any high-risk factor(s) that can potentially make them a candidate for a spiritual miscarriage?

    ❑ Spiritual Maturity   ❑ Spiritual Dysfunctions   ❑ Paternal Traits
    ❑ Spiritual Trauma and Infections   ❑ Medications   ❑ Spiritual Diet
    ❑History of Spiritual Miscarriages   ❑ Toxin Environment   ❑_____

3. If, so can you explain your diagnoses

    _____
    _____
    _____
    _____
    _____
    _____
    _____
    _____

4. Based upon your patient chart can you identify signs of a potential spiritual miscarriage?

    ❑ Yes ❑No

5. If so, what was the signs?

    ❑ Spiritual Ignorance   ❑Spiritual Bleeding   ❑Spiritual Torment

6. Diagnose any infections that could contribute to your patient having a spiritual miscarriage.

    _____   _____   _____

    _____   _____   _____

    _____   _____   _____

Explain your spiritual miscarriage infection diagnoses for your patient.

_____
_____
_____
_____
_____
_____
_____

Prenatal Aftercare Treatment

Can you provide your patient with medical after care advice that would assist them from having a spiritual miscarriage?

_____
_____
_____
_____
_____
_____
_____

Prescription Scripture (s)

_____
_____
_____
_____
_____
_____
_____

Reflections:

Can you recall a time where you compromised your belief because you didn't want to be gossip about because them? ❑ Yes ❑No?

If so, what lead you to compromise? How did it make you feel afterward? Was it worth it?

_____
_____
_____
_____
_____
_____

What lessons can you take away from Joseph to apply in your own life or situation?

_____
_____
_____
_____
_____
_____
_____

Patient Chart
Eve

Scripture Study: Genesis 3

Vital Statistics

- **Location Lived:** Garden of Eden
- **Career:** Wife, helper, companion, co-manager of Eden
- **Family:** Husband: Adam. Sons: Cain, Abel, Seth. Numerous other children.

Immunizations:

- _____
- _____
- _____
- _____
- _____

Infections/Diseases/ Allergies:

- _____
- _____
- _____
- _____
- _____
- _____

Physical History:

- _____
- _____
- _____

Lab work: Ordered Test:

- _____
- _____
- _____
- _____
- _____

Confidential Patient Notes:

_____
_____
_____
_____
_____
_____
_____
_____
_____
_____
_____
_____
_____
_____
_____
_____
_____
_____
_____
_____
_____
_____
_____
_____

Lab Work Results:

- _____
  _____
- _____
  _____
- _____
  _____
- _____
  _____

Prenatal Diagnoses

1. Was your patient a likely candidate for a spiritual miscarriage? ❑ Yes ❑No

2. Can you identify any high-risk factor that could cause your patient to have a spiritual miscarriage?

   ❑ Spiritual Maturity   ❑ Spiritual Dysfunctions   ❑ Paternal Traits
   ❑ Spiritual Trauma and Infections   ❑ Medications   ❑ Spiritual Diet
   ❑History of Spiritual Miscarriages   ❑ Toxin Environment   ❑ _____

3. If, so can you explain your diagnoses

   _____
   _____
   _____
   _____
   _____
   _____
   _____
   _____

4. Based upon your patient chart can you identify signs of a potential spiritual miscarriage?

   ❑ Yes ❑No

5. If so, what was the signs?

   ❑ Spiritual Ignorance   ❑Spiritual Bleeding   ❑Spiritual Torment

6. Chart the areas of infections that are warning signs of a spiritual miscarriage

   _____   _____   _____
   _____   _____   _____
   _____   _____   _____

Explain you diagnoses.

_____
_____
_____
_____
_____
_____
_____

Prenatal Aftercare Treatment

Can you provide the patient with medical after care advice that would assist them from having a spiritual miscarriage?

_____
_____
_____
_____
_____
_____
_____

Prescription Scripture (s)

_____
_____
_____
_____
_____
_____

Reflections:

Have you ever been in a place where your desires called you to be disobedient to the word of God? ❑ Yes ❑No

If so, what desire enticed you to sin? How did it make you feel afterward? Was it worth it?

_____
_____
_____
_____
_____
_____

What lessons can you take away from Eve to apply in your own life or situation?

_____
_____
_____
_____
_____
_____
_____

Patient Chart
Abraham

Scripture Study: Genesis 20[DZ2]

Vital Statistics

- **Location Lived:** Born in Ur of the Chaldeans; spent most of his life in the land of Canaan
- **Career:** Wealthy livestock owner
- **Family:** Father: Terah. Brothers: Nahor and Haran. Wife: Sarah. Nephew: Lot. Sons: Ishmael and Isaac.
- **Social group:** Abimelech, Melchizedek

Immunizations:

- **Faith:** Left his father and everything behind and followed God
- **Respect:** Esteemed by others
- **Courage:** Rescued Lot from exile
- **Hospitality:** Took his nephew lot with him and took care of him
- **Success:** Wealthy in livestock, silver, and gold
- **Entrepreneurship:** Livestock owner
- **Peace maker:** Pursued peace between himself and Lot
- **Leader:** Gathered up an army and lead them to victory in war

Infections/Diseases/ Allergies:

- **Liar:** Said that Sarai was his wife
- **Selfish:** Was willing to let Sarai be sexually abused, commit adultery, and dishonored for the sake of his own life. Had no thought about her consequences
- **Deception:** Led Sarah to believe that the lie was for her, own good.
- **Thief:** Took things from Pharaoh under false pretense
- **Faithless:** When famine came in Canaan, he went to Egypt instead of going to God.
- **Adultery:** Slept with Hagar
- **Fear:** was afraid that he, would be killed because of his beautiful wife

Physical History[DZ3]:

Abram was a man challenged by God to believe, trust, and have faith in Him. God tested him to leave everything that was known, unto him and called him to an unfamiliar place with the promise that He will make him a great nation and bless him. Abram took God up on the offer and left everything that God requested of Him. After leaving he had many challenges of his faith in between the prophetic word of God and the promise. Abram faced famine, eviction, death, compromise, scandals, lies and so much more that tested and perfected his faith. Through his walk, he found areas where his faith was weak and had to strengthen during the journey. Abram journey was training him how to walk faithfully before God. We find Abram in the time of trouble seeing his own way through that lead him into more trouble than it was worth because he depended on himself. Even through his self-dependency, he found that God was faithful. When Abram, failed or stumbled God would always bail him out.

Lab work: Ordered Test:

- Trust & Faith in God
- Made a great nation
- Name made great
- Be a blessing to others
- Father of many nations

Confidential Patient Notes:

_____
_____
_____
_____
_____
_____
_____
_____
_____
_____
_____
_____
_____
_____
_____
_____
_____
_____
_____
_____
_____
_____
_____
_____

Lab Work Results: [DZ4]

- _____
  _____
- _____
  _____
- _____
  _____
- _____
  _____

Prenatal Diagnoses

1. Was patient a likely candidate for a spiritual miscarriage? ❑ Yes ❑No

2. Can your patient be diagnosed with any high-risk factor(s) that can potentially make them a candidate for a spiritual miscarriage?

    ❑ Spiritual Maturity   ❑ Spiritual Dysfunctions   ❑ Paternal Traits
    ❑ Spiritual Trauma and Infections   ❑ Medications   ❑ Spiritual Diet
    ❑History of Spiritual Miscarriages   ❑ Toxin Environment   ❑_____

3. If, so can you explain your diagnoses

    _____
    _____
    _____
    _____
    _____
    _____
    _____
    _____

4. Based upon your patient chart can you identify signs of a potential spiritual miscarriage?

    ❑ Yes ❑No

5. If so, what was the signs?

    ❑ Spiritual Ignorance   ❑Spiritual Bleeding   ❑Spiritual Torment

6. Chart the areas of infections that are warning signs for a spiritual miscarriage

    _____   _____   _____
    _____   _____   _____
    _____   _____   _____

    Explain you diagnoses.

    _____
    _____
    _____
    _____
    _____
    _____
    _____

Prenatal Aftercare Treatment

Can you provide your patient with medical after care advice that would assist them from having a spiritual miscarriage?

_____
_____
_____
_____
_____
_____
_____
_____

Prescription Scripture (s)

_____
_____
_____
_____
_____
_____
_____

Reflections:

Can you recall a time where you omitted seeking the guidance of God and did things on your own accord? ❑ Yes ❑No

Did God come and bail you out? Was it worth it?

_____
_____
_____
_____
_____
_____
_____

What lessons can you take away from Abram to apply in your own life or situation?

_____
_____
_____
_____
_____
_____
_____

Patient Chart
Haman

Scripture Study: Read Esther 3   **Person**: Haman

[DZ5]**Vital Statistics**

- **Location Lived:** Susa, the capital of Persia
- **Career:** Second in rank in the empire
- **Family**: Wife: Zeresh
- **Social group:** Xerxes, Mordecai, Esther

Immunizations:

- _____
- _____
- _____
- _____
- _____

Infections/Diseases/ Allergies:

- _____
- _____
- _____
- _____
- _____
- _____

Physical History:

- _____
- _____
- _____

Lab work: Ordered Test:

- _____
- _____
- _____
- _____
- _____

Confidential Patient Notes:

_____
_____
_____
_____
_____
_____
_____
_____
_____
_____
_____
_____
_____
_____
_____
_____
_____
_____
_____
_____
_____
_____
_____

Lab Work Results:

- _____
_____
- _____
_____
- _____
_____
- _____
_____

Prenatal Diagnoses

1. Can your patient be considered as a spiritual miscarriage patient? ❑ Yes ❑No

2. Explain your diagnoses.

   _____
   _____
   _____
   _____
   _____
   _____
   _____
   _____

3. Does your patient have any signs that could put them at high-risk of having a spiritual miscarriage? ❑ Yes ❑No

4. If so, chart the signs you have identified.

❑ Spiritual Maturity	❑ Spiritual Dysfunctions	❑ Paternal Traits
❑ Spiritual Trauma and Infections	❑ Medications	❑ Spiritual Diet
❑History of Spiritual Miscarriages	❑ Toxin Environment	❑_____

5. Provide an explanation of your patient risk factors.

   _____
   _____
   _____
   _____
   _____
   _____
   _____
   _____

6. Is your patient currently having a spiritual miscarriage? ❑ Yes ❑No

7. If so, what sign(s) assisted you with your patient analyzes?

   ❑ Spiritual Ignorance   ❑Spiritual Bleeding   ❑Spiritual Torment

8. Chart your patient symptoms that could lead to a spiritual miscarriage

   _____   _____   _____
   _____   _____   _____
   _____   _____   _____

Prenatal Aftercare Treatment

Can you provide medical advice that would assist someone else that are having the same symptoms as your patient from having a spiritual miscarriage?

_____
_____
_____
_____
_____
_____
_____
_____

Prescription Scripture (s)

_____
_____
_____
_____
_____
_____
_____

Reflections:

Has your pride ever caused you to loss something(s)? ❏ Yes ❏No

If so, what was it? What built the wall of pride? How did it make you feel afterward? Was it worth it?

_____
_____
_____
_____
_____
_____
_____

What lessons can you take away from Haman to apply in your own life or situation?

_____
_____
_____
_____
_____
_____
_____

Patient Chart
Hannah

Scripture Study: Read 1 Samuel 1

Vital Statistics

- **Location Lived:** Ephraim
- **Career:** Homemaker
- **Family:** Husband: Elkanah. Son: Samuel. Later, three other sons and two daughters.
- **Social group**: Eli the priest

Immunizations:

- _____
- _____
- _____
- _____
- _____

Infections/Diseases/ Allergies:

- _____
- _____
- _____
- _____
- _____
- _____

Physical History:

- _____
- _____
- _____

Lab work: Ordered Test:

- _____
- _____
- _____
- _____
- _____

Confidential Patient Notes:

_____
_____
_____
_____
_____
_____
_____
_____
_____
_____
_____
_____
_____
_____
_____
_____
_____
_____
_____
_____
_____
_____

Lab Work Results:

- _____
_____
- _____
_____
- _____
_____
- _____
_____

Prenatal Diagnoses

1. Can your patient be considered as a spiritual miscarriage patient? ❏ Yes ❏No

2. Explain your diagnoses any symptoms.

   _____
   _____
   _____
   _____
   _____
   _____

3. Does your patient have any signs that could put them at high-risk of having a spiritual miscarriage? ❏ Yes ❏No

4. If so, chart the signs you have identified.

❏ Spiritual Maturity	❏ Spiritual Dysfunctions	❏ Paternal Traits
❏ Spiritual Trauma and Infections	❏ Medications	❏ Spiritual Diet
❏History of Spiritual Miscarriages	❏ Toxin Environment	❏ _____

5. Provide an explanation of your patient risk factors.

   _____
   _____
   _____
   _____
   _____
   _____

6. Is your patient currently having a spiritual miscarriage? ❏ Yes ❏No

7. If so, what sign(s) assisted you with your patient analyzes?
   ❏ Spiritual Ignorance   ❏Spiritual Bleeding   ❏Spiritual Torment

8. Chart the symptoms that could lead to a spiritual miscarriage

   _____   _____   _____
   _____   _____   _____
   _____   _____   _____

Prenatal Aftercare Treatment

Provide your patient with medical advice after care that would assist them from having a spiritual miscarriage.

_____
_____
_____
_____
_____
_____

Prescription Scripture (s)

_____
_____
_____
_____
_____
_____

Reflections:

Have you ever rejected the pure love of someone because of the void or anguish you felt within? ❑ Yes ❑No

What was you longing for that caused you to reject their love? What was the outcome? How straining was it in the relationship? What are you doing now to overcome that void?

_____
_____
_____
_____
_____

What lessons can you take away from Hannah to apply in your own life or situation?

_____
_____
_____
_____
_____
_____

Patient Chart

_____

Put your name here

Scripture Study: Your Life

Vital Statistics

- **Location Lived:** _____
- **Career:** _____
- **Family:** _____
  _____
- **Social group:** _____
  _____

Immunizations:

- _____
- _____
- _____
- _____
- _____

Infections/Diseases/ Allergies:

- _____
- _____
- _____
- _____
- _____

Physical History:

- _____
- _____

Lab work: Ordered Test:

- _____
- _____
- _____
- _____
- _____

Confidential Patient Notes:

_____
_____
_____
_____
_____
_____
_____
_____
_____
_____
_____
_____
_____
_____
_____
_____
_____
_____
_____
_____
_____
_____

Lab Work Results:

- _____
  _____
- _____
  _____
- _____
  _____
- _____
  _____

Prenatal Diagnoses

1. Can you be considered as a spiritual miscarriage patient? ❑ Yes ❑No

2. Explain your diagnoses.

   _____

   _____

   _____

   _____

   _____

   _____

   _____

   _____

3. Do you have any signs that that would consider you being a high-risk patient for having a spiritual miscarriage? ❑ Yes ❑No

4. If so, chart the signs you can identified.

   ❑ Spiritual Maturity   ❑ Spiritual Dysfunctions   ❑ Paternal Traits
   ❑ Spiritual Trauma and Infections   ❑ Medications   ❑ Spiritual Diet
   ❑History of Spiritual Miscarriages   ❑ Toxin Environment   ❑_____

5. Provide an explanation of her warning signs.

   _____

   _____

   _____

   _____

   _____

   _____

   _____

   _____

6. Have you previously had a spiritual miscarriage(s)? ❑ Yes ❑No

7. What caused your spiritual miscarriage?

   ❑ Spiritual Ignorance   ❑Spiritual Bleeding   ❑Spiritual Torment

8. What infection signs can you identify that is causing your spiritual miscarriage

   _____   _____   _____

   _____   _____   _____

   _____   _____   _____

Prenatal Aftercare Treatment

Provide your patient with medical advice after care that would assist them from having a spiritual miscarriage.

_____
_____
_____
_____
_____
_____
_____

Prescription Scripture (s)

_____
_____
_____
_____
_____
_____

Reflections:

_____
_____
_____
_____
_____
_____
_____
_____
_____
_____
_____
_____
_____
_____
_____
_____
_____
_____
_____

Spiritual Abortion

Fear of God will cause you to **FULFILL** your destiny

and the Fear of man will cause you to **ABORT** your destiny

But he who received the seed on stony places, this is he who hears the word and immediately receives it with joy; yet he has no root in himself, but endures only for a while. For when tribulation or persecution arises because of the word, immediately he stumbles. *Matthew 13:20-21 (NKJV)*

Patient Chart
Adonijah

Study Scripture: 1 King 1-2

- **Location Lived:** Hebron
- **Career:** Prince
- **Family:** Father: David. Mother: Haggith. Half-brothers: Amnon, Kileab, Absalom, Solomon, and others. Half Sister: Tamar.
- **Social group:** Joab, Abiathar, Jonathan, Charioteers

Immunizations:

- **Leader:** He knew how to gain the support of others to follow him
- **Assertive:** He went after what he desired
- **Bold:** he was a risk taker

Infections/Diseases/ Allergies:

- **Pride:** He felt his look, charisma and his birthing position gained him kingship rights
- **Deception:** Plotted to get what he wanted
- **Lack of Discipline:** He was spoiled and allowed to do what he wanted with no penalties
- **Disloyalty:** Went back on his word
- **Rebellious:** Attempted to take over the kingdom
- **Arrogance:** Felt that he was the most qualified to be king despite God's choice
- **Self-Exaltation:** Appointed himself to kingship
- **Fear:** Thought he was about the die because of his revolt against the kings
- **Covetousness:** Desired kingship at any cost

Physical History:

Adonijah was King David fourth son a prince to the throne of Israel. He has been involved in a few traumatic episodes, that caused shock, grief, and disturbance in his life. He experienced watching the death of his brother, the crown prince Amnon at the command of his brother Absalom. *2 Samuel 13:28*. In addition, he along with the rest of his brothers had to flee for their lives, because they thought it was in jeopardy. *2 Samuel 13:29*. They considered that their brother had in mind to kill all of them. Adonijah was never disciplined by his father, throughout his life. Which produced an attitude, where he did what he wanted in regard, to how it affected others. He has no consciousness of repercussions behind his actions. Therefore, it influenced his lack of self-control, disrespectful and rebellious behavior. That eventually, lead to his revolt to take the kingdom.

Lab work: Ordered Test:

- **Abandonment**: Renounce his claims to the throne
- **Righteousness**: No wickedness found in him
- **Loyalty:** Prove himself to be a loyal man

Confidential Patient Notes:

Adonijah, next in line, positional to be king but not chosen by God. Not happy with God plan and wanting what he wants he took matters into his own hands.

Adonijah, the opportunist, decided to take advantage of his father bedridden illness and rebel. In his rebellious state, he covets the throne of Israel and exalts himself as king. When his father, King David's hears about the revolt. He quickly put God plan into action by placing Solomon king over Israel. Due to Adonijah revolt, he could have been put to death for his treason, unto the king. The newly establish King Solomon, showing mercy gave Adonijah the opportunity to live if he would renounce his claims to the throne and find himself to be loyal to him. Needing the time to reorganize how he would take kingship, Adonijah, agreed with his mouth but he still coveted the throne in his heart. Obtaining no consequence behind his action aided in him staying in his old patterns of behaviors.

Adonijah was very persistent in obtaining the royal throne comes up with a new plot on becoming the king over Israel. His new revised plan to become king was to gain his father concubine Abishag hand in marriage. If he, could pull off this deception it would position him to making claims to the royal throne. With the aid of his counselors, Joab and Abiathar in this decision gave him confidence that it would work. He meets with Bathsheba desiring a consolation of marriage to Abishag for King Solomon taking his place in kingship. With pity for him, Bathsheba agrees to speak with her son on his behalf.

Adonijah was hoping to take advantage of King Solomon deep respect for his mother. He thought that the King would grant any request from his mother. Bathsheba unaware of his plot, goes before the King and asks for Abishag to be given to Adonijah as his wife. King Solomon, denies the request of his mother. Full of wisdom the king knew that the request came from Abishag and it was a part of a bigger skim to come after the throne of Israel. Therefore, Adonijah request caused him to have an abortion as it showed he could not prove himself to be loyal and he was still seeking kingship. It triggered the following consequences

Lab Work Results:

- **Termination of life**: King Solomon enrage due to the disloyalty and deception of Adonijah immediately pronounced his execution.

Prenatal Diagnoses

1. Can your patient be considered as a spiritual abortion candidate? ❑ Yes ❑No

2. Explain your diagnoses.

_____
_____
_____
_____
_____
_____
_____

3. Have you identified any high-risk factors that could trigger a spiritual abortion for your patient? ❑ Yes ❑No

4. If so, chart the signs you have identified.

❑ Spiritual Maturity   ❑ Spiritual Dysfunctions   ❑ Paternal Traits
❑ Spiritual Trauma and Infections   ❑ Medications   ❑ Spiritual Diet
❑History of Spiritual Abortions   ❑ Toxin Environment   ❑_____

5. Provide an explanation of the events(s) that led to these high-risk signs for your patient.

_____
_____
_____
_____
_____
_____
_____

6. Is your patient currently having a spiritual abortion? ❑ Yes ❑No

7. If so, what sign(s) assisted you with your patient analyzes?

❑ Spiritual Ignorance   ❑Spiritual Bleeding   ❑Spiritual Torment

8. Chart the symptoms that you have detected that caused your patient to have a spiritual abortion

_____   _____   _____
_____   _____   _____
_____   _____   _____

Prenatal Aftercare Treatment

Provide the patient with medical advice after care that would assist someone else from having a spiritual abortion.

_____
_____
_____
_____
_____
_____
_____

Prescription Scripture (s)

_____
_____
_____
_____
_____
_____

Reflections:

Have you ever backstabbed someone to take their position, their mate, or anything that they had? ❑ Yes ❑No

What was your purpose behind backstabbing them? How did it make you feel afterward? Was it worth it?

_____
_____
_____
_____
_____
_____

What lessons can you take away from Adonijah to apply in your own life or situation?

_____
_____
_____
_____
_____
_____

Patient Chart
Eliphaz, Bildad , and Zophar

[DZ6]**Study Scripture: Job 2-26**

Vital Statistics

- **Location Lived:** Uz
- **Social group:** Job, Elihu

Immunizations:

- **Knowledgeable:** They knew the word of God
- **Supportive:** They came to sympathize and comfort job.
- **Loyal:** They attended to Job when he was in isolation.
- **Unity:** They mourned and grieved as one with Job
- **Genuine Friendship:** They stood with Job in his suffering
- **Concern:** The came to check on Job.
- **Patience:** They sat with him for seven days.
- **Stillness:** They set in silence for 7 days

Infections/Diseases/ Allergies:

- **Discouragement:** Did not uplift job in the situation
- **Prideful:** They wanted to be right
- **Judgmental:** Assumed job suffering as a punishment for sin.
- **Offensive:** Had issues with job not agreeing with their allegations
- **Abusive:** Continually use the word incorrectly to bring condemnation upon Job
- **Lacked Wisdom:** Decided to try to explain Job's suffering rather than help him endure it
- **Accusation:** Claimed that Job had to sin
- **Dismissive:** Dismissed Jobs expression of grief

Physical History:

Eliphaz, Bildad, and Zophar were true friends of Job. When they heard about what had taken place, they departed from their busy lives to come and attend to Job. The men traveled from various parts of the country taking travel expenses. They were authentic in their relationship as they took the time to be attentive unto Job. These men had to have love Job as they risked being contamination to be with him during his lost and suffering.

Lab work: Ordered Test:

- Console their friend through grief

Confidential Patient Notes:

_____
_____
_____
_____
_____
_____
_____
_____
_____
_____
_____
_____
_____
_____
_____
_____
_____
_____
_____
_____
_____
_____
_____
_____

Lab Work Results:

- _____
  _____
- _____
  _____
- _____
  _____
- _____
  _____

Prenatal Diagnoses

1. Is your patient a spiritual abortion candidate? ❑ Yes ❑No

2. Explain your diagnoses.

   _____
   _____
   _____
   _____
   _____
   _____
   _____
   _____

3. Have you identified any high-risk factors that could cause your patient to have a spiritual abortion? ❑ Yes ❑No

4. If so, chart the signs you have identified.

   ❑ Spiritual Maturity   ❑ Spiritual Dysfunctions   ❑ Paternal Traits
   ❑ Spiritual Trauma and Infections   ❑ Medications   ❑ Spiritual Diet
   ❑ History of Spiritual Abortions   ❑ Toxin Environment   ❑_____

5. Provide an explanation of your patient risk factors.

   _____
   _____
   _____
   _____
   _____
   _____
   _____

6. Is your patient currently having a spiritual abortion? ❑ Yes ❑No

7. If so, what sign(s) assisted you with your patient analyzes?

   ❑ Spiritual Ignorance   ❑Spiritual Bleeding   ❑Spiritual Torment

8. Chart your diagnoses that is leading your patient to having a spiritual abortion

   _____   _____   _____
   _____   _____   _____
   _____   _____   _____

Prenatal Aftercare Treatment

Provide patient with medical advice after care that would assist them from having a spiritual abortion.

_____
_____
_____
_____
_____
_____
_____

Prescription Scripture (s)

_____
_____
_____
_____
_____
_____
_____

Reflections:

Have God ever sent you on assignment to comfort a friend in their time of suffering, grief, or lost?   ❑ Yes ❑No Explain what happen Could you find some of Jobs friend characteristics in you?

_____
_____
_____
_____
_____
_____
_____

What lessons can you take away from Job's friend to apply in your own life or situation?

_____
_____
_____
_____
_____
_____
_____

Patient Chart
Korah

Scripture Study[DZ7]: Numbers 16

Vital Statistics

- **Location Lived:** Egypt, Sinai peninsula
- **Career:** Levite (Tabernacle assistant)
- **Family:** Father: Izhar Brothers: Nepheg, and Zichri.
- **Social group:** Dathan, Abiram, and On

Immunizations:

- **Leadership**: Had the ability to influence others to follow him.

Infections/Diseases/ Allergies:

- **Pride:** Thought that he desired to be priest over Israel.
- **Covetousness:** Desired to be priesthood and organize a rebellion to take it.
- **Division:** Caused men to come against their leaders
- **Greed:** What God had given was not enough he wanted what the priest had.
- **Wrath**: Came against Moses and Aaron leadership
- **Anger**: Upset because he was not in
- **Blame**: Accused Moses for them not entering the promise land
- **Ungrateful**: Failed to recognize the significant position God had given him

Physical History:

Korah an influential leader of Israel from tribe of Levite. He underwent oppression under the Kingship of Pharaoh in Egypt. Karoh experienced God's deliverance and salvation from the Egyptian. When God opened the Rea Sea, he walked between it on dry ground. He saw God consistently defeat kingdoms on their behalf, provide food, shelter and water for them, and so much more. Korah was a part of the rebellion against God about the promise land. In addition, he was appointed by God to special service in the Tabernacle.

Lab work: Ordered Test:

- Assisted in the daily functions of the Tabernacle

Confidential Patient Notes:

_____
_____
_____
_____
_____
_____
_____
_____
_____
_____
_____
_____
_____
_____
_____
_____
_____
_____
_____
_____
_____
_____
_____

Lab Work Results:

- _____
  _____
- _____
  _____
- _____
  _____
- _____
  _____

Prenatal Diagnoses

1. Is your patient a likely candidate for consideration for as a spiritual abortion? ❑ Yes ❑No

2. Explain your diagnoses.

_____
_____
_____
_____
_____
_____

3. Have you identified any high-risk factors that could cause your patient to have a spiritual abortion? ❑ Yes ❑No

4. If so, chart the signs you have identified.

❑ Spiritual Maturity   ❑ Spiritual Dysfunctions ❑ Paternal Traits
❑ Spiritual Trauma and Infections ❑ Medications   ❑ Spiritual Diet
❑History of Spiritual Abortions ❑ Toxin Environment   ❑_____

5. Provide an explanation of your patient risk factors.

_____
_____
_____
_____
_____
_____

6. Is your patient currently having a spiritual abortion? ❑ Yes ❑No

7. If so, what sign(s) assisted you with your patient analyzes?

❑ Spiritual Ignorance   ❑Spiritual Bleeding   ❑Spiritual Torment

8. Chart the symptoms that could aid your patient into having spiritual abortion.

_____ _____ _____
_____ _____ _____
_____ _____ _____

Prenatal Aftercare Treatment

Can you provide medical advice that would assist someone else that are having the same symptoms as your patient from having a spiritual abortion?

_____
_____
_____
_____
_____
_____
_____

Prescription Scripture (s)

_____
_____
_____
_____
_____
_____
_____

Reflections:

Have God given you a position that you are not content with because you are so busy looking at what some else have? ❑ Yes ❑No Write down what it is and why you desire what they have.

_____
_____
_____
_____
_____
_____

What lessons can you take away from Korah to apply in your own life or situation?

_____
_____
_____
_____
_____
_____
_____

```
┌─────────────────────────────────────┐
│           Patient Chart              │
│              Saul                    │
└─────────────────────────────────────┘
```

Scripture Study: 1 Samuel 15

[DZ8]**Vital Statistics**

- **Career:** King of Israel
- **Location Lived:** The land of Benjamin
- **Family:** Father: Kish. Wife: Ahinoam. Sons: Jonathan, Malkishua, Abinadab, Ishbosheth (and possibly Ishvi). Daughters: Merab, Michal.
- **Social group:** Samuel

Immunizations:

- _____
- _____
- _____
- _____
- _____

Infections/Diseases/ Allergies:

- _____
- _____
- _____
- _____
- _____
- _____

Physical History:

- _____
- _____
- _____

Lab work: Ordered Test:

- _____
- _____
- _____
- _____
- _____

Confidential Patient Notes:

_____
_____
_____
_____
_____
_____
_____
_____
_____
_____
_____
_____
_____
_____
_____
_____
_____
_____
_____
_____
_____
_____

Lab Work Results:

- _____
_____
- _____
_____
- _____
_____
- _____
_____

Prenatal Diagnoses

1. Can patient be considered as a spiritual abortion candidate? ❏ Yes ❏No

2. Explain your diagnoses.

   _____
   _____
   _____
   _____
   _____
   _____
   _____
   _____

3. Have you identified any high-risk factors that could cause your patient to have a spiritual abortion? ❏ Yes ❏No

4. If so, chart the signs you have identified.

   ❏ Spiritual Maturity   ❏ Spiritual Dysfunctions   ❏ Paternal Traits
   ❏ Spiritual Trauma and Infections   ❏ Medications   ❏ Spiritual Diet
   ❏History of Spiritual Abortions   ❏ Toxin Environment   ❏_____

5. Provide an explanation of your patient risk factors.

   _____
   _____
   _____
   _____
   _____
   _____
   _____

6. Is your patient currently having a spiritual abortion? ❏ Yes ❏No

7. If so, what sign(s) assisted you with your patient analyzes?
   ❏ Spiritual Ignorance   ❏Spiritual Bleeding   ❏Spiritual Torment

8. Chart the areas of infections that could lead to a spiritual abortion for your patient

   _____   _____   _____
   _____   _____   _____
   _____   _____   _____

Prenatal Aftercare Treatment

Provide your patient with medical advice after care that would assist them from having a spiritual abortion.

_____
_____
_____
_____
_____

Prescription Scripture (s)

_____
_____
_____
_____
_____

Reflections:

Have you ever listened and did what other people wanted you in spite of what you should have done? ❑ Yes ❑No

Why did you follow others then what you knew to do? Identify your risk factors and infections that lead to your behavior?

_____
_____
_____
_____
_____

Are there things that you should have started and you have not because of what others have said or lack of support? ❑ Yes ❑No Are you planning to start? ❑ Yes ❑No   Why or why not

_____
_____
_____
_____

What lessons can you take away from your patient to apply in your own life or situation?

_____
_____
_____
_____

Patient Chart
Esau

Scripture Study[DZ9]: Genesis 25:27-34

Vital Statistics

- **Location Lived:** Canaan
- **Career:** Skillful hunter
- **Family:** Parents: Isaac and Rebekah. Brother: Jacob. Wives: Judith, Basemath, and Mahalath.

Immunizations:

- _____
- _____
- _____
- _____
- _____

Infections/Diseases/ Allergies:

- _____
- _____
- _____
- _____
- _____
- _____

Physical History:

- _____
- _____
- _____

Lab work: Ordered Test:

- _____
- _____
- _____
- _____
- _____

Confidential Patient Notes:

_____
_____
_____
_____
_____
_____
_____
_____
_____
_____
_____
_____
_____
_____
_____
_____
_____
_____
_____
_____
_____
_____

Lab Work Results:

- _____
  _____
- _____
  _____
- _____
  _____
- _____
  _____

Prenatal Diagnoses

1. Can your patient be considered as a spiritual abortion candidate? ❑ Yes ❑No

2. Explain your diagnoses.

_____
_____
_____
_____
_____
_____
_____
_____

3. What high-risk factors have you identified that could cause your patient to have a spiritual abortion? ❑ Yes ❑No

4. If so, chart the signs you have identified.

❑ Spiritual Maturity   ❑ Spiritual Dysfunctions   ❑ Paternal Traits
❑ Spiritual Trauma and Infections   ❑ Medications   ❑ Spiritual Diet
❑History of Spiritual Abortions   ❑ Toxin Environment   ❑_____

5. Provide an explanation of your patient risk factors.

_____
_____
_____
_____
_____
_____
_____
_____

6. Is your patient currently having a spiritual abortion? ❑ Yes ❑No

7. If so, what sign(s) assisted you with your patient analyzes?

❑ Spiritual Ignorance   ❑Spiritual Bleeding   ❑Spiritual Torment

8. Chart the areas of infections that could lead to a spiritual abortion for your patient.

_____   _____   _____
_____   _____   _____
_____   _____   _____

Prenatal Aftercare Treatment

Provide your patient with medical advice after care that would assist them from having a spiritual abortion.

_____
_____
_____
_____
_____
_____
_____
_____

Prescription Scripture (s)

_____
_____
_____
_____
_____
_____
_____

Reflections:

Have you ever settled for instant gratification and did something without thinking or caring about the consequence? ❏ Yes ❏No What are the high-risk factors that contributed to your decision?

_____
_____
_____
_____
_____
_____
_____

What lessons can you take away from Esau to apply in your own life or situation?

_____
_____
_____
_____
_____
_____
_____

Patient Chart
Rehoboam

Scripture Study: [DZ10]

Vital Statistics

- **Location Lived:** Jerusalem
- **Career:** King of the united kingdom of Israel and later of the southern kingdom of Judah
- **Family:** Father: Solomon. Mother: Naamah. Wife: Maacah. Son: Abijah.
- **Social group:** Jeroboam, Shishak, Shemaiah

Immunizations:

- _____
- _____
- _____
- _____
- _____

Infections/Diseases/ Allergies:

- _____
- _____
- _____
- _____
- _____
- _____

Physical History:

- _____
- _____
- _____

Lab work: Ordered Test:

- _____
- _____
- _____
- _____
- _____

Confidential Patient Notes:

_____
_____
_____
_____
_____
_____
_____
_____
_____
_____
_____
_____
_____
_____
_____
_____
_____
_____
_____
_____
_____

Lab Work Results:

- _____
  _____
- _____
  _____
- _____
  _____
- _____
  _____

Prenatal Diagnoses

1. Is your patient a spiritual abortion candidate? ❑ Yes ❑No

2. Explain your diagnoses.

   _____
   _____
   _____
   _____
   _____
   _____
   _____
   _____

3. Have you identified any high-risk factors that could cause your patient to have a spiritual abortion? ❑ Yes ❑No

4. If so, chart the signs you have identified.

   ❑ Spiritual Maturity   ❑ Spiritual Dysfunctions   ❑ Paternal Traits
   ❑ Spiritual Trauma and Infections   ❑ Medications   ❑ Spiritual Diet
   ❑History of Spiritual Abortions   ❑ Toxin Environment   ❑_____

5. Provide an explanation of your patient risk factors.

   _____
   _____
   _____
   _____
   _____
   _____
   _____

6. Is your patient currently having a spiritual abortion? ❑ Yes ❑No

7. If so, what sign(s) assisted you with your patient analyzes?

   ❑ Spiritual Ignorance   ❑Spiritual Bleeding   ❑Spiritual Torment

8. Chart the areas of infections that is jeopardizing your patient from delivering their assignment.

   _____   _____   _____
   _____   _____   _____
   _____   _____   _____

Prenatal Aftercare Treatment

Provide patient with medical advice after care that would assist them from having a spiritual abortion.

_____
_____
_____
_____
_____
_____
_____

Prescription Scripture (s)

_____
_____
_____
_____
_____
_____
_____

Reflections:

Have you ever listen to bad counsel that caused you more trouble than good? ❏ Yes ❏No

Why did you listen to them? What advice would your future self, tell your past self about the situation?

_____
_____
_____
_____
_____
_____

What lessons can you take away from Rehoboam to apply in your own life or situation?

_____
_____
_____
_____
_____
_____

Patient Chart
Jeremiah

Scripture Study: [DZ11] Jeremiah 20:7-18

Vital statistics

- **Location Lived:** Anathoth
- **Career**: Prophet
- **Family**: Father: Hilkiah
- **Social group**: Josiah, Jehoahaz, Jehoiakim, Jehoiachin, Zedekiah, Baruch

Immunizations:

- _____
- _____
- _____
- _____
- _____

Infections/Diseases/ Allergies:

- _____
- _____
- _____
- _____
- _____
- _____

Physical History:

- _____
- _____
- _____

Lab work: Ordered Test:

- _____
- _____
- _____
- _____
- _____

Confidential Patient Notes:

_____
_____
_____
_____
_____
_____
_____
_____
_____
_____
_____
_____
_____
_____
_____
_____
_____
_____
_____
_____
_____
_____
_____
_____

Lab Work Results:

- _____
  _____
- _____
  _____
- _____
  _____
- _____
  _____

Prenatal Diagnoses

1. Can your patient be considered as a spiritual abortion candidate? ❑ Yes ❑No

2. Explain your diagnoses.

   _____
   _____
   _____
   _____
   _____
   _____
   _____
   _____

3. What high-risk factors have you identified that could contribute to your patient having a spiritual abortion? ❑ Yes ❑No

4. If so, chart the signs you have identified.

   ❑ Spiritual Maturity   ❑ Spiritual Dysfunctions   ❑ Paternal Traits
   ❑ Spiritual Trauma and Infections   ❑ Medications   ❑ Spiritual Diet
   ❑History of Spiritual Abortions   ❑ Toxin Environment   ❑_____

5. Provide an explanation of your patient risk factors.

   _____
   _____
   _____
   _____
   _____
   _____
   _____
   _____

6. Is your patient currently having a spiritual abortion? ❑ Yes ❑No

7. If so, what sign(s) assisted you with your patient analyzes?

   ❑ Spiritual Ignorance   ❑Spiritual Bleeding   ❑Spiritual Torment

8. Chart the areas of infections that could lead to a spiritual abortion for your patient.

   _____   _____   _____
   _____   _____   _____
   _____   _____   _____

Prenatal Aftercare Treatment

Provide your patient with medical advice after care that would assist them from having a spiritual abortion.

_____
_____
_____
_____
_____
_____
_____

Prescription Scripture (s)

_____
_____
_____
_____
_____
_____
_____

Reflections:

Have you ever been so hurt, disappointed and just wanted to give up because you were being picked on, abused, talked about, accused, etc.? ❑ Yes ❑No What are the high-risk factors that contributed to those feelings?

_____
_____
_____
_____
_____
_____

What lessons can you take away from Jeremiah to apply in your own life or situation?

_____
_____
_____
_____
_____
_____

Patient Chart
King Solomon

Scripture Study: Read *1 King 11:9-26* [DZ12]

Vital statistics

- **Location Lived:** Jerusalem
- **Career**: King of Israel
- **Family**: Father: David. Mother: Bathsheba. Brothers: Absalom, Adonijah. Sister: Tamar. Son: Rehoboam.

Immunizations:

- _____
- _____
- _____
- _____
- _____

Infections/Diseases/ Allergies:

- _____
- _____
- _____
- _____
- _____
- _____

Physical History:

- _____
- _____
- _____

Lab work: Ordered Test:

- _____
- _____
- _____
- _____
- _____

Confidential Patient Notes:

_____
_____
_____
_____
_____
_____
_____
_____
_____
_____
_____
_____
_____
_____
_____
_____
_____
_____
_____
_____
_____
_____

Lab Work Results:

- _____
- _____
- _____
- _____

Prenatal Diagnoses

1. Can your patient be considered as a spiritual abortion candidate? ❏ Yes ❏No

2. Explain your diagnoses.

     _____
     _____
     _____
     _____
     _____
     _____
     _____
     _____

3. What high-risk factors have you identified that could cause your patient to have a spiritual abortion? ❏ Yes ❏No

4. If so, chart the signs you have identified.

     ❏ Spiritual Maturity   ❏ Spiritual Dysfunctions   ❏ Paternal Traits
     ❏ Spiritual Trauma and Infections   ❏ Medications   ❏ Spiritual Diet
     ❏History of Spiritual Abortions   ❏ Toxin Environment   ❏_____

5. Provide an explanation of your patient warning signs.

     _____
     _____
     _____
     _____
     _____
     _____
     _____
     _____

6. Is your patient currently having a spiritual abortion? ❏ Yes ❏No

7. If so, what sign(s) assisted you with your patient analyzes?

     ❏ Spiritual Ignorance   ❏Spiritual Bleeding   ❏Spiritual Torment

8. Chart the areas of infections that could lead to a spiritual abortion for your patient.

     _____   _____   _____
     _____   _____   _____
     _____   _____   _____

Prenatal Aftercare Treatment

Provide your patient with medical advice after care that would assist them from having a spiritual abortion.

_____
_____
_____
_____
_____
_____
_____

Prescription Scripture (s)

_____
_____
_____
_____
_____
_____
_____

Reflections:

Have you ever been around associates that corrupted your morals? ❑ Yes ❑No

What are the high-risk factors that contributed to your decision?

_____
_____
_____
_____
_____
_____
_____

What lessons can you take away from King Solomon to apply in your own life or situation?

_____
_____
_____
_____
_____
_____
_____

Patient Chart
Hophni & Phinehas

Scripture Study: Read 1 Samuel 2 & 1 Samuel 4

Vital Statistics

- **Location Lived:** Shiloh
- **Careers:** High priest, judge of Israel
- **Family:** Father: Eli
- **Social group:** Samuel

Immunizations:

- _____
- _____
- _____
- _____
- _____

Infections/Diseases/ Allergies:

- _____
- _____
- _____
- _____
- _____
- _____

Physical History:

- _____
- _____
- _____

Lab work: Ordered Test:

- _____
- _____
- _____
- _____
- _____

Confidential Patient Notes:

_____
_____
_____
_____
_____
_____
_____
_____
_____
_____
_____
_____
_____
_____
_____
_____
_____
_____
_____
_____
_____
_____

Lab Work Results:

- _____
_____
- _____
_____
- _____
_____
- _____
_____

Prenatal Diagnoses

1. Can your patient be considered as a spiritual abortion candidate? ❑ Yes ❑No

2. Explain your diagnoses.

_____

_____

_____

_____

_____

_____

_____

_____

3. What high-risk factors have you identified that could cause your patient to have a spiritual abortion? ❑ Yes ❑No

4. If so, chart the signs you have identified.

❑ Spiritual Maturity   ❑ Spiritual Dysfunctions   ❑ Paternal Traits
❑ Spiritual Trauma and Infections   ❑ Medications   ❑ Spiritual Diet
❑History of Spiritual Abortions   ❑ Toxin Environment   ❑_____

5. Provide an explanation of your patient warning signs.

_____

_____

_____

_____

_____

_____

_____

6. Is your patient currently having a spiritual abortion? ❑ Yes ❑No

7. If so, what sign(s) assisted you with your patient analyzes?

❑ Spiritual Ignorance   ❑Spiritual Bleeding   ❑Spiritual Torment

8. Chart the symptoms that could lead to a spiritual abortion for your patient.

_____   _____   _____

_____   _____   _____

_____   _____   _____

Prenatal Aftercare Treatment

Provide medical advice that would prevent a patient with a similar from having a spiritual abortion.

_____
_____
_____
_____
_____
_____
_____
_____

Prescription Scripture (s)

_____
_____
_____
_____
_____
_____
_____
_____

Reflections:

Have you ever found yourself being unfaithful to your assignment, purpose, dreams, etc? ❑ Yes ❑No

What are the high-risk factors that contributed to your decision?

_____
_____
_____
_____
_____
_____
_____

What lessons can you take away from Hophni & Phinehas to apply in your own life or situation?

_____
_____
_____
_____
_____
_____
_____
_____

Patient Chart

_____

Put your name here

Scripture Study: Your Life

Vital Statistics

- **Location Lived:** _____
- **Career:** _____
- **Family:** _____
  _____
- **Social group:** _____
  _____

Immunizations:

- _____
- _____
- _____
- _____
- _____

Infections/Diseases/ Allergies:

- _____
- _____
- _____
- _____
- _____

Physical History:

- _____
- _____

Lab work: Ordered Test:

- _____
- _____
- _____
- _____
- _____

Confidential Patient Notes:

_____
_____
_____
_____
_____
_____
_____
_____
_____
_____
_____
_____
_____
_____
_____
_____
_____
_____
_____
_____
_____

Lab Work Results:

- _____
  _____
- _____
  _____
- _____
  _____
- _____
  _____

Prenatal Diagnoses

1. Can you be considered as a spiritual abortion patient? ❑ Yes ❑No

2. Explain your diagnoses.

   _____
   _____
   _____
   _____
   _____
   _____
   _____
   _____

3. Do you have any signs that that would consider you being a high-risk patient for having a spiritual abortion? ❑ Yes ❑No

4. If so, chart the signs you can identified.

   ❑ Spiritual Maturity   ❑ Spiritual Dysfunctions   ❑ Paternal Traits
   ❑ Spiritual Trauma and Infections   ❑ Medications   ❑ Spiritual Diet
   ❑History of Spiritual Abortions   ❑ Toxin Environment   ❑_____

5. Provide an explanation of her warning signs.

   _____
   _____
   _____
   _____
   _____
   _____
   _____
   _____

6. Have you previously had a spiritual abortion(s)? ❑ Yes ❑No

7. What caused your spiritual abortion?

   ❑ Spiritual Ignorance   ❑Spiritual Bleeding   ❑Spiritual Torment

8. What infection signs can you identify that is causing your spiritual abortion

   _____   _____   _____
   _____   _____   _____
   _____   _____   _____

Prenatal Aftercare Treatment

Provide your patient with medical advice after care that would assist them from having a spiritual abortion.

_____
_____
_____
_____
_____
_____

Prescription Scripture (s)

_____
_____
_____
_____
_____

Reflections:

_____
_____
_____
_____
_____
_____
_____
_____
_____
_____
_____
_____
_____
_____
_____
_____

Spiritual Stillborn

Fear of God will cause you to fulfill your destiny and

Fear of man will cause you to abort your destiny

The one who received the seed that fell among the thorns is the man who hears the word, but the worries of this life and the deceitfulness of wealth choke it, making it unfruitful. *Matthew 13:22 (NIV)*

Patient Chart
Hagar

Scripture Study: Genesis 16:6

Vital Statistics

- **Location Lived:** Canaan and Egypt
- **Career:** Servant, mother
- **Family:** Son: Ishmael

Strength and accomplishment

- **Servant:** Was a servant unto Sarai
- **Faithful:** Served Sarai through the famine, war, and eviction
- **Humble:** had to submit unto

Infections/Diseases/ Allergies:

- **Pride:** She begin to despise Sarai after becoming pregnant.
- **Adultery:** Sleep with Sarai husband
- **Malice:** Despise Sarai after becoming pregnant and choosing her to sleep with her husband
- **Abuse:** She was treated harshly by Sarai
- **Haughty:** Was not submitted to Sarai
- **Misused:** Used by Sarai to bring her a child
- **Hurt:** Trust of a friend broken

Physical History

Hagar is a slave under Abram household. She was the maidservant of Sarai who responsibilities were to tend to her needs. She served Sarai through many phases of their lives in their time of peace, war, chaos, famine, evictions, etc. Tending to Sarai must have created a bond between them that was very close. Out of this bond, Sarai had conversations with Hagar about how much she loved Abram and her desire to give him a child. Points of discussions could have included Gods promise to Abram as well as her frustration and disappointment of not yet conceiving. Hagar being faithful encourage Sarai as she tended to her as she wiped away the tears of disappointment when Sarai patience of conceiving would fail. Hagar served Sarai physically and emotionally. Her mistress being impatient and gave up on conceiving a child for Abram. Instead of keeping the faith she devised her own plan that included Hagar being a surrogate mother for them. Sarai must have chosen her because of the bond that they had acquired through her years of serving.

Lab work: Ordered Test:
- **Servant:** Serve as Sarai maidservant

Confidential Patient Notes:

Hagar wakes up one day and finds herself in a very unpleasant and uncomfortable situation. She became a part of Sarai plan to bring forth a child for them when she realized she passed child barren age. Out of all their servants somehow, she became the chosen vessel. She wasn't asked to be a surrogate mother for Sarai she was just given to Abram without any consent. Hagar was in Abram household to serve the needs of Sarai. She had no idea that her servanthood would be extended to sleeping with her mistress husband. This must have made Hagar feel uncomfortable, angry, misused, and degraded as she found herself under Abram. Sarai plan was successful as Hagar conceived a child for Abram.

This situation hurt the relationship between Hagar and Sarai as it put an emotional strain on them both. Feeling very betrayed Hagar begin to express her feelings outwardly toward her mistress. Sarai, also seeing the Abram newly found attitude toward Hagar stirred up jealousy, resentment, anger, disappointment in her. Hagar's mistress confronts Abram, about her and he left the situation in the hand of his broken hearted, jealous, angry wife. Sarai took this authority and begin to treat Hagar very harshly.

At this point, Hagar's life under Sarai's hand was hostile and threatening to even the baby she carried. Without any options available to correct Sarai's behavior she considered that it was in her best interest to run away. Her pain, shame, and anger suffocated her compassionate servanthood. As well as, Sarai behavior choked Hagar's compacity to serve her pleasantly due to harsh treatment. Hagar has terminated her assignment to serve Sarai and found herself in the desert pregnant, alone and hurt

Lab Work Results:

- **Abused**: Mistreated by Sarai
- **Angered:** Upset because of the harsh treatment she is receiving
- **Hurt:** betrayed and mistreated by someone she tended and cared
- **Abandon:** No one would come to the rescue of her mistreatment
- **Violated:** Did not ask to be a part of Sarai plan but was included with out consent
- **Broken relationships:** negatively affected Hagar relationship with Sarai and Abram.
- **Avoidance**: Runs away from the problem instead of facing it.

Prenatal Diagnoses

1. Can your patient be considered as a spiritual stillborn candidate? ❑ Yes ❑No

2. Explain your diagnoses.

   _____
   _____
   _____
   _____
   _____
   _____
   _____
   _____

3. Have you diagnosed any high-risk factors that could cause your patient to have a spiritual stillborn? ❑ Yes ❑No

4. If so, chart the signs you have identified.

   ❑ Spiritual Maturity   ❑ Spiritual Dysfunctions   ❑ Paternal Traits
   ❑ Spiritual Trauma and Infections ❑ Medications   ❑ Spiritual Diet
   ❑History of Spiritual Stillbirths   ❑ Toxin Environment   ❑_____

5. Provide an explanation of your patient risk factors.

   _____
   _____
   _____
   _____
   _____
   _____
   _____
   _____

6. Is your patient currently having a spiritual stillborn? ❑ Yes ❑No

7. If so, what sign(s) aided you with your patient analyzes?

   ❑ Spiritual Ignorance   ❑Spiritual Bleeding   ❑Spiritual Torment

8. Chart the symptoms that could lead to a spiritual stillborn for your patient

   _____   _____   _____
   _____   _____   _____
   _____   _____   _____

Prenatal Aftercare Treatment

Provide your patient with medical advice after care that would assist them from having a spiritual stillborn.

_____

_____

_____

_____

_____

Prescription Scripture (s)

_____

_____

_____

_____

_____

Reflections:

Have you ever been treated so badly that you quit your assignment? ❏ Yes ❏No What led you to that decision? How would you have handled it differently?

_____

_____

_____

_____

_____

_____

_____

What lessons can you take away from Hagar to apply in your own life or situation?

_____

_____

_____

_____

_____

_____

_____

Patient Chart
Zerubbabel & Israelites

Scripture Study: Ezra 4

Vital Statistics [DZ13][DZ14]

- **Location Lived:** Babylon, Jerusalem
- **Career:** Governor of Judah
- **Family:** Father: Shealtiel. Grandfather: Jehoiachin.
- **Social group:** Cyrus, Darius, Zechariah, Haggai

Immunizations:

- **Leader:** Led Israel from exile to Jerusalem and in the rebuilding of the temple
- **Trust:** Trusted the word of God
- **Wisdom:** Consulted God and others before making decision
- **Coachable:** Open to advice
- **Accountable:** Took ownership of his responsibility.
- **Trustworthy:** Was given the treasury and articles of the temple
- **Motivated:** Heard the word of God and moved in it. Did not care about the cost.
- **Sacrificial:** Left comfortable to do hard work
- **Organizer:** Hired the people necessary to get the resources to build the temple
- **Hard worker:** Hands on with the work. Often led in the required work
- **Worshiper:** Started the rebuilding with worship

Infections/Diseases/ Allergies:

- **Discourage:** He needed to be encouraged during the challenging times
- **Stagnation:** Allows adversity to halt the rebuilding
- **Frustration:** When the people stop the work got frustrated and complacent.
- **Weary:** Couldn't keep the people motivated in the work to keep them moving

Physical History:

Zerubbabel was an exile in Babylon. He was born as a slave in Persia and a survivor of Israel's ancestors, who was brought into captivity. With restricted freedom, I'm sure Zerubbabel made the best of the situation and still lead within his boundaries. During the Israelites captivity, the Lord used the Babylonians to destroy Jerusalem and the temple of God. And the time has arisen for the word of Jeremiah to be fulfilled of Gods people being brought out of captivity. Zerubbabel, a leader of Israel who was charged with leading the procession of Isreal's exile back home to Jerusalem to rebuild the temple of God. How exciting it must be to lead your people out of exile and back into the place of God's promise. Zerubbabel chose among many with much zeal to lead in the possession and the rebuilding. He started his race very motivated and encouraged with this esteemed honor. He was responsible for leading the Israelites back to Jerusalem successful. After, settling in their homes, he along with others rebuilt the altar of God and begun making scarifies unto Him. He orchestrated getting the people hired and paid for what was necessary for the assignment. Then finally they started the rebuilding of the temple of God. Zerubbabel took his assignment seriously as he did not delay in getting the people and things in place to do the work that was required to bring the word of God to pass.

Lab work: Ordered Test:

- **Skilled**: Go up to Jerusalem in Judah and build the temple of the LORD
- **Leadership**: Lead in the rebuilding of the temple

Confidential Patient Notes:

_____
_____
_____
_____
_____
_____
_____
_____
_____
_____
_____
_____
_____
_____
_____
_____
_____
_____
_____
_____
_____
_____

Lab Work Results:

- _____
  _____
- _____
  _____
- _____
  _____
- _____
  _____

Prenatal Diagnoses

1. Can your patient be considered as a spiritual stillborn candidate? ❑ Yes ❑No

2. Explain your diagnoses.

   _____
   _____
   _____
   _____
   _____
   _____
   _____

3. Have you identified any high-risk factors that could cause your patient to have a spiritual stillborn? ❑ Yes ❑No

4. If so, chart the signs you have identified.

   ❑ Spiritual Maturity   ❑ Spiritual Dysfunctions   ❑ Paternal Traits
   ❑ Spiritual Trauma and Infections   ❑ Medications   ❑ Spiritual Diet
   ❑History of Spiritual stillbirths   ❑ Toxin Environment   ❑_____

5. Provide an explanation of your patient risk factors.

   _____
   _____
   _____
   _____
   _____
   _____
   _____

6. Is your patient currently at risk of having a spiritual stillborn? ❑ Yes ❑No

   ❑ Spiritual Ignorance   ❑Spiritual Bleeding   ❑Spiritual Torment

7. Chart the areas of infections that could lead to a spiritual stillborn for your patient

   _____   _____   _____
   _____   _____   _____
   _____   _____   _____

Prenatal Aftercare Treatment

Provide your patient with medical advice after care that would assist them from having a spiritual stillborn.

_____
_____
_____
_____
_____
_____
_____

Prescription Scripture (s)

_____
_____
_____
_____
_____

Reflections:

Have you ever started doing something for God and stop because you became discourage due to everything that was coming up against you? ❏ Yes ❏No

How did the enemy discourage you? Go find scriptures in the word of God that speaks to those areas. Have you started back in the assignment? ❏ Yes ❏No If, not set a date to start and begin the work again. Start Date: _____

_____
_____
_____
_____
_____
_____

What lessons can you take away from Zerubbabel to apply in your own life or situation?

_____
_____
_____
_____
_____
_____

Patient Chart
Tamar

Scripture Study: 2 Samuel 13:20

Vital Statistics

- **Location Lived:** Hebron
- **Career:** Princess of Israel
- **Family:** Parents: David & Maacah Brother: Absalom Half-Brother: Amnon, , Solomon, Adonijah and others

Immunizations:

- _____
- _____
- _____
- _____
- _____

Infections/Diseases/ Allergies:

- _____
- _____
- _____
- _____
- _____

Physical History:

_____
_____
_____
_____
_____

Lab work: Ordered Test:

- _____
- _____
- _____
- _____
- _____

Confidential Patient Notes:

_____
_____
_____
_____
_____
_____
_____
_____
_____
_____
_____
_____
_____
_____
_____
_____
_____
_____
_____
_____
_____
_____

Lab Work Results:

- _____
  _____
- _____
  _____
- _____
  _____
- _____
  _____

Prenatal Diagnoses

1. Can your patient be considered as a spiritual stillborn candidate? ❑ Yes ❑No

2. Explain your diagnoses.

   _____
   _____
   _____
   _____
   _____
   _____
   _____
   _____

3. Have you identified any high-risk factors that could cause your patient to have a spiritual stillborn? ❑ Yes ❑No

4. If so, chart the signs you have identified.

   ❑ Spiritual Maturity   ❑ Spiritual Dysfunctions ❑ Paternal Traits
   ❑ Spiritual Trauma and Infections ❑ Medications   ❑ Spiritual Diet
   ❑History of Spiritual Stillbirths ❑ Toxin Environment ❑_____

5. Provide an explanation of your patient risk factors.

   _____
   _____
   _____
   _____
   _____
   _____
   _____
   _____

6. Is your patient currently having a spiritual stillborn? ❑ Yes ❑No

7. If so, what sign(s) assisted you with your patient analyzes?

   ❑ Spiritual Ignorance ❑Spiritual Bleeding ❑Spiritual Torment

8. Chart the symptoms that could lead to a spiritual stillborn for your patient

   _____ _____ _____
   _____ _____ _____
   _____ _____ _____

Prenatal Aftercare Treatment

Provide your patient with medical advice after care that would assist them from having a spiritual stillborn.

_____
_____
_____
_____
_____
_____
_____
_____

Prescription Scripture (s)

_____
_____
_____
_____
_____
_____
_____

Reflections:

Are there areas in your life that you have shut off or suppress because of the trauma from past abuse? ❑ Yes ❑No

Name those areas? How can you overcome them?

_____
_____
_____
_____
_____
_____
_____

What lessons can you take away from Tamar to apply in your own life or situation?

_____
_____
_____
_____
_____
_____
_____

Patient Chart
Young Prophet

Scripture Study: 1 King 13:13-19

Vital Statistics

- **Location Lived:** Judah
- **Career:** Prophet of God
- **Family:** N/A
- **Social group:** Jeroboam, old prophet

Immunizations:

- _____
- _____
- _____
- _____
- _____

Infections/Diseases/ Allergies:

- _____
- _____
- _____
- _____
- _____

Physical History:

_____
_____
_____
_____
_____

Lab work: Ordered Test:

- _____
- _____
- _____
- _____
- _____

Confidential Patient Notes:

_____
_____
_____
_____
_____
_____
_____
_____
_____
_____
_____
_____
_____
_____
_____
_____
_____
_____
_____
_____
_____
_____

Lab Work Results:

- _____
  _____
- _____
  _____
- _____
  _____
- _____
  _____

Prenatal Diagnoses

1. Can your patient be considered as a spiritual stillborn candidate? ❑ Yes ❑No

2. Explain your diagnoses.

   _____

   _____

   _____

   _____

   _____

   _____

   _____

   _____

3. Have you identified any high-risk factors that could cause your patient to have a spiritual stillborn? ❑ Yes ❑No

4. If so, chart the signs you have identified.

   ❑ Spiritual Maturity   ❑ Spiritual Dysfunctions   ❑ Paternal Traits

   ❑ Spiritual Trauma and Infections   ❑ Medications   ❑ Spiritual Diet

   ❑History of Spiritual Stillbirths   ❑ Toxin Environment   ❑_____

5. Provide an explanation of your patient risk factors.

   _____

   _____

   _____

   _____

   _____

   _____

   _____

   _____

6. Is your patient currently having a spiritual stillborn? ❑ Yes ❑No

7. If so, what sign(s) assisted you with your patient analyzes?

   ❑ Spiritual Ignorance   ❑Spiritual Bleeding   ❑Spiritual Torment

8. Chart the symptoms that could lead to a spiritual stillborn for your patient

   _____   _____   _____

   _____   _____   _____

   _____   _____   _____

Prenatal Aftercare Treatment

Provide your patient with medical advice after care that would assist them from having a spiritual stillborn.

_____
_____
_____
_____
_____

Prescription Scripture (s)

_____
_____
_____
_____
_____

Reflections:

Have you trusted someone else word over the word of God? ❑ Yes ❑No How did it or has it turned out for you?

_____
_____
_____
_____
_____

Have you ever buried the word of God on the inside of you because of what someone else have said or because of what you thought others might think?

_____
_____
_____
_____
_____

What lessons can you take away from the Young Prophet to apply in your own life or situation?

_____
_____
_____
_____
_____

Patient Chart
Achan

Scripture Study: Read Joshua 7:1- -8:2

Vital Statistics

- **Location Lived:** Wilderness of Sinai
- **Career:** fighting man of Jerusalem
- **Family:** Father: Carmi

Immunizations:

- _____
- _____
- _____
- _____
- _____

Infections/Diseases/ Allergies:

- _____
- _____
- _____
- _____
- _____
- _____

Physical History:

_____
_____
_____
_____
_____

Lab work: Ordered Test:

- _____
- _____
- _____
- _____
- _____

Confidential Patient Notes:

_____
_____
_____
_____
_____
_____
_____
_____
_____
_____
_____
_____
_____
_____
_____
_____
_____
_____
_____
_____
_____

Lab Work Results:

- _____
  _____
- _____
  _____
- _____
  _____
- _____
  _____

Prenatal Diagnoses

1. Can your patient be considered as a spiritual stillborn candidate? ❑ Yes ❑No

2. Explain your diagnoses.

   _____
   _____
   _____
   _____
   _____
   _____
   _____
   _____

3. Have you identified any high-risk factors that could cause your patient to have a spiritual stillborn? ❑ Yes ❑No

4. If so, chart the signs you have found.

   ❑ Spiritual Maturity   ❑ Spiritual Dysfunctions   ❑ Paternal Traits
   ❑ Spiritual Trauma and Infections   ❑ Medications   ❑ Spiritual Diet
   ❑History of Spiritual Stillbirths   ❑ Toxin Environment   ❑_____

5. Provide an explanation of your patient risk factors.

   _____
   _____
   _____
   _____
   _____
   _____
   _____
   _____

6. Is your patient currently having a spiritual stillborn? ❑ Yes ❑No

7. If so, what sign(s) helped you with your patient analyzes?

   ❑ Spiritual Ignorance   ❑Spiritual Bleeding   ❑Spiritual Torment

8. Chart the areas of infections that could lead to a spiritual stillborn for your patient

   _____   _____   _____
   _____   _____   _____
   _____   _____   _____

Prenatal Aftercare Treatment

Provide your patient with medical advice after care that would assist them from having a spiritual stillborn.

_____
_____
_____
_____
_____
_____
_____

Prescription Scripture (s)

_____
_____
_____
_____
_____
_____
_____
_____

Reflections:

Have you ever been so focus on what someone else have that it caused you to miss out on what God had awaiting you? ❑ Yes ❑No[DZ15]

What drew your attention to those things? How have you or can you overcome this distraction ?

_____
_____
_____
_____
_____
_____
_____

What lessons can you take away from Achan to apply in your own life or situation?

_____
_____
_____
_____
_____
_____
_____

```
┌─────────────────────────────────────────────┐
│              Patient Chart                    │
│                                               │
│                 Jacob                         │
│                                               │
└─────────────────────────────────────────────┘
```

[DZ16]**Scripture Study:** Genesis[DZ17]

Vital Statistics

- **Location Lived:** Canaan
- **Career:** Shepherd, livestock owner
- **Family:** Parents: Isaac and Rebekah. Brother: Esau. Father-in-law: Laban. Wives: Rachel and Leah. Offspring: Twelve sons and one daughter are mentioned in the Bible.

Immunizations:

- _____
- _____
- _____
- _____
- _____

Infections/Diseases/ Allergies:

- _____
- _____
- _____
- _____
- _____
- _____

Physical History:

_____
_____
_____
_____
_____

Lab work: Ordered Test:

- _____
- _____
- _____
- _____
- _____
```
```

Confidential Patient Notes:

_____
_____
_____
_____
_____
_____
_____
_____
_____
_____
_____
_____
_____
_____
_____
_____
_____
_____
_____
_____
_____
_____

Lab Work Results:

- _____
  _____
- _____
  _____
- _____
  _____
- _____
  _____

Prenatal Diagnoses

1. Can your patient be considered as a spiritual stillborn candidate? ❑ Yes ❑No

2. Explain your diagnoses.

_____
_____
_____
_____
_____
_____
_____
_____

3. Have you identified any high-risk factors that could cause your patient to have a spiritual stillborn? ❑ Yes ❑No

4. If so, chart the signs you have identified.

   ❑ Spiritual Maturity   ❑ Spiritual Dysfunctions   ❑ Paternal Traits
   ❑ Spiritual Trauma and Infections   ❑ Medications   ❑ Spiritual Diet
   ❑History of Spiritual Stillbirths   ❑ Toxin Environment   ❑_____

5. Provide an explanation of your patient risk factors.

_____
_____
_____
_____
_____
_____
_____
_____

6. Is your patient currently having a spiritual stillborn? ❑ Yes ❑No

7. If so, what sign(s) assisted you with your patient analyzes?

   ❑ Spiritual Ignorance   ❑Spiritual Bleeding   ❑Spiritual Torment

8. Chart the symptoms that could lead to a spiritual stillborn for your patient

_____   _____   _____
_____   _____   _____
_____   _____   _____

Prenatal Aftercare Treatment

Provide your patient with medical advice after care that would assist them from having a spiritual stillborn.

_____
_____
_____
_____
_____
_____
_____

Prescription Scripture (s)

_____
_____
_____
_____
_____
_____
_____

Reflections:

Have you ever been in a place where you were not able to grow and mature in your calling because you were too preoccupied working on other things or too busy serving others? ❑ Yes ❑No

How did or how can you bring balance?

_____
_____
_____
_____
_____
_____

What lessons can you take away from Jacob to apply in your own life or situation?

_____
_____
_____
_____
_____
_____
_____

Patient Chart

ELI [DZ18]

Study Scriptures: 1 Samuel 3:11-14

Vital Statistics

- **Location Lived:** Shiloh
- **Careers**: High priest, judge of Israel
- **Family:** Sons: Hophni and Phinehas
- **Social group**: Samuel

Immunizations:

- _____
- _____
- _____
- _____
- _____

Infections/Diseases/ Allergies:

- _____
- _____
- _____
- _____
- _____
- _____

Physical History:

_____
_____
_____
_____
_____

Lab work: Ordered Test:

- _____
- _____
- _____
- _____
- _____

Confidential Patient Notes:

_____
_____
_____
_____
_____
_____
_____
_____
_____
_____
_____
_____
_____
_____
_____
_____
_____
_____
_____
_____
_____

Lab Work Results:

- _____
  _____
- _____
  _____
- _____
  _____
- _____
  _____

9. Can your patient be considered as a spiritual stillborn candidate? ❑ Yes ❑No

10. Explain your diagnoses.

_____

_____

_____

_____

_____

_____

_____

_____

11. Have you identified any high-risk factors that could cause your patient to have a spiritual stillborn? ❑ Yes ❑No

12. If so, chart the signs you have identified.

❑ Spiritual Maturity   ❑ Spiritual Dysfunctions   ❑ Paternal Traits
❑ Spiritual Trauma and Infections   ❑ Medications   ❑ Spiritual Diet
❑History of Spiritual Stillbirths   ❑ Toxin Environment   ❑_____

13. Provide an explanation of your patient risk factors.

_____

_____

_____

_____

_____

_____

_____

_____

14. Is your patient currently having a spiritual stillborn? ❑ Yes ❑No

15. If so, what sign(s) assisted you with your patient analyzes?

❑ Spiritual Ignorance   ❑Spiritual Bleeding   ❑Spiritual Torment

16. Chart the areas of infections that could lead to a spiritual stillborn for your patient

_____ _____ _____

_____ _____ _____

_____ _____ _____

Prenatal Aftercare Treatment

Provide your patient with medical advice after care that would assist them from having a spiritual stillborn.

_____
_____
_____
_____
_____
_____
_____
_____

Prescription Scripture (s)

_____
_____
_____
_____
_____
_____
_____

Reflections:

Have you been silent when you should have spoken out?   ❑ Yes ❑No[DZ19]

What risk factors or infections keep you from speaking out? How did it make you feel afterward?

_____
_____
_____
_____
_____
_____
_____

What lessons can you take away from Eli to apply in your own life or situation?

_____
_____
_____
_____
_____
_____
_____

Patient Chart
Cain

Scripture Study: Genesis 4:7

[DZ20] **Vital Statistics**

- **Location Lived:** Near Eden, which was probably located in present-day Iraq or Iran
- **Career:** Farmer, then wanderer
- **Family:** Parents: Adam and Eve. Brothers: Abel, Seth, and others not mentioned by name.

Immunizations:

- _____
- _____
- _____
- _____
- _____

Infections/Diseases/ Allergies:

- _____
- _____
- _____
- _____
- _____
- _____

Physical History:

_____
_____
_____
_____
_____

Lab work: Ordered Test:

- _____
- _____
- _____
- _____
- _____

Confidential Patient Notes:

_____

_____

_____

_____

_____

_____

_____

_____

_____

_____

_____

_____

_____

_____

_____

_____

_____

_____

_____

_____

_____

_____

Lab Work Results:

- _____

_____

- _____

_____

- _____

_____

- _____

_____

Prenatal Diagnoses

1. Can your patient be considered as a spiritual stillborn candidate? ❏ Yes ❏No

2. Explain your diagnoses.

   _____
   _____
   _____
   _____
   _____
   _____
   _____
   _____

3. Have you identified any high-risk factors that could cause your patient to have a spiritual stillborn? ❏ Yes ❏No

4. If so, chart the signs you have identified.

   ❏ Spiritual Maturity   ❏ Spiritual Dysfunctions   ❏ Paternal Traits
   ❏ Spiritual Trauma and Infections ❏ Medications   ❏ Spiritual Diet
   ❏History of Spiritual Stillbirths ❏ Toxin Environment   ❏_____

5. Provide an explanation of your patient risk factors.

   _____
   _____
   _____
   _____
   _____
   _____
   _____
   _____

6. Is your patient currently having a spiritual stillborn? ❏ Yes ❏No

7. If so, what sign(s) assisted you with your patient analyzes?

   ❏ Spiritual Ignorance   ❏Spiritual Bleeding   ❏Spiritual Torment

8. Chart the areas of infections that could lead to a spiritual stillborn for your patient

   _____   _____   _____
   _____   _____   _____
   _____   _____   _____

Prenatal Aftercare Treatment

Provide your patient with medical advice after care that would assist them from having a spiritual stillborn.

_____
_____
_____
_____
_____
_____
_____

Prescription Scripture (s)

_____
_____
_____
_____
_____
_____
_____

Reflections:

Have you ever regretted something you did out of anger? ❏ Yes ❏No

What factors and/or infections that you can identify that triggered your behavior?

_____
_____
_____
_____
_____
_____
_____

What lessons can you take away from Cain to apply in your own life or situation?

_____
_____
_____
_____
_____
_____
_____

Patient Chart
Asa

[DZ21]**Study Scripture:** 1 Kings 15:8-24 and 2 Chronicles 14-16.[DZ22]

Vital Statistics
- **Location Lived:** Jerusalem
- **Career:** King of Judah
- **Family:** Grandmother: Maacah. Father: Abijah. Son: Jehoshaphat.
- **Social group:** Hanani, Ben-hadad, Zerah, Azariah, Baasha

Immunizations:

- _____
- _____
- _____
- _____
- _____

Infections/Diseases/ Allergies:

- _____
- _____
- _____
- _____
- _____
- _____

Physical History:

_____
_____
_____
_____
_____
_____

Lab work: Ordered Test:

- _____
- _____
- _____
- _____
- _____

Confidential Patient Notes:

_____
_____
_____
_____
_____
_____
_____
_____
_____
_____
_____
_____
_____
_____
_____
_____
_____
_____
_____
_____
_____
_____

Lab Work Results:

- _____
  _____
- _____
  _____
- _____
  _____
- _____
  _____

Prenatal Diagnoses

1. Can your patient be considered as a spiritual stillborn candidate? ❑ Yes ❑No

2. Explain your diagnoses.

   _____
   _____
   _____
   _____
   _____
   _____
   _____
   _____

3. Have you identified any high-risk factors that could cause your patient to have a spiritual stillborn? ❑ Yes ❑No

4. If so, chart the signs you have identified.

   ❑ Spiritual Maturity   ❑ Spiritual Dysfunctions   ❑ Paternal Traits
   ❑ Spiritual Trauma and Infections ❑ Medications   ❑ Spiritual Diet
   ❑History of Spiritual Stillbirths ❑ Toxin Environment   ❑_____

5. Provide an explanation of your patient risk factors.

   _____
   _____
   _____
   _____
   _____
   _____
   _____
   _____

6. Is your patient currently having a spiritual stillborn? ❑ Yes ❑No

7. If so, what sign(s) assisted you with your patient analyzes?

   ❑ Spiritual Ignorance   ❑Spiritual Bleeding   ❑Spiritual Torment

8. Chart the symptoms that could lead to a spiritual stillborn for your patient

   _____   _____   _____
   _____   _____   _____
   _____   _____   _____

Prenatal Aftercare Treatment

Provide your patient with medical advice after care that would assist them from having a spiritual stillborn.

_____
_____
_____
_____
_____
_____
_____

Prescription Scripture (s)

_____
_____
_____
_____
_____
_____
_____

Reflections:

Have you ever trusted in people or other things more than you have God? ❑ Yes ❑No

What factors caused you to trust in them or it over God?

_____
_____
_____
_____
_____
_____
_____

What lessons can you take away from Asa to apply in your own life or situation?

_____
_____
_____
_____
_____
_____
_____

Patient Chart
Balaam

Scripture study[DZ23][DZ24]

Vital Statistics

- **Location Lived:** Lived near the Euphrates River, traveled to Moab
- **Careers**: Sorcerer, prophet
- **Family**: Father: Beor
- **Social group:** Balak (king of Moab), Moses, Aaron

Immunizations:

- _____
- _____
- _____
- _____
- _____

Infections/Diseases/ Allergies:

- _____
- _____
- _____
- _____
- _____
- _____

Physical History:

_____
_____
_____
_____
_____

Lab work: Ordered Test:

- _____
- _____
- _____
- _____
- _____

Confidential Patient Notes:

_____
_____
_____
_____
_____
_____
_____
_____
_____
_____
_____
_____
_____
_____
_____
_____
_____
_____
_____
_____
_____
_____

Lab Work Results:

- _____
_____
- _____
_____
- _____
_____
- _____
_____

Prenatal Diagnoses

1. Can your patient be considered as a spiritual stillborn candidate? ❑ Yes ❑No

2. Explain your diagnoses.

_____
_____
_____
_____
_____
_____
_____
_____

3. Have you identified any high-risk factors that could cause your patient to have a spiritual stillborn? ❑ Yes ❑No

4. If so, chart the signs you have identified.

❑ Spiritual Maturity	❑ Spiritual Dysfunctions	❑ Paternal Traits
❑ Spiritual Trauma and Infections	❑ Medications	❑ Spiritual Diet
❑History of Spiritual Stillbirths	❑ Toxin Environment	❑_____

5. Provide an explanation of your patient risk factors.

_____
_____
_____
_____
_____
_____
_____
_____

6. Is your patient currently having a spiritual stillborn? ❑ Yes ❑No

7. If so, what sign(s) assisted you with your patient analyzes?

❑ Spiritual Ignorance   ❑Spiritual Bleeding   ❑Spiritual Torment

8. Chart the areas of infections that could lead to a spiritual stillborn for your patient

_____   _____   _____
_____   _____   _____
_____   _____   _____

Prenatal Aftercare Treatment

Provide your patient with medical advice after care that would assist them from having a spiritual stillborn.

_____
_____
_____
_____
_____
_____
_____
_____

Prescription Scripture (s)

_____
_____
_____
_____
_____
_____
_____
_____

Reflections:

Have you ever perverted your gifts from God? ❑ Yes ❑No

If so, what factors led to your perverting your gifts? How did it make you feel afterward? Was it worth it?

_____
_____
_____
_____
_____
_____
_____

What lessons can you take away from Balaam to apply in your own life or situation?

_____
_____
_____
_____
_____
_____
_____

Patient Chart

_____

Put your name here

Scripture Study: Your Life

Vital Statistics

- **Location Lived:** _____
- **Career:** _____
- **Family:** _____
  _____
- **Social group:** _____
  _____

Immunizations:

- _____
- _____
- _____
- _____
- _____

Infections/Diseases/ Allergies:

- _____
- _____
- _____
- _____
- _____

Physical History:

- _____
- _____

Lab work: Ordered Test:

- _____
- _____
- _____
- _____
- _____

Confidential Patient Notes:

_____
_____
_____
_____
_____
_____
_____
_____
_____
_____
_____
_____
_____
_____
_____
_____
_____
_____
_____
_____
_____
_____

Lab Work Results:

- _____
  _____
- _____
  _____
- _____
  _____
- _____
  _____

Prenatal Diagnoses

9. Can you be considered as a spiritual abortion patient? ❑ Yes ❑No

10. Explain your diagnoses.

    _____
    _____
    _____
    _____
    _____
    _____
    _____
    _____

11. Do you have any signs that that would consider you being a high-risk patient for having a spiritual abortion? ❑ Yes ❑No

12. If so, chart the signs you can identified.

    ❑ Spiritual Maturity   ❑ Spiritual Dysfunctions   ❑ Paternal Traits
    ❑ Spiritual Trauma and Infections   ❑ Medications   ❑ Spiritual Diet
    ❑History of Spiritual Abortions   ❑ Toxin Environment   ❑_____

13. Provide an explanation of her warning signs.

    _____
    _____
    _____
    _____
    _____
    _____
    _____
    _____

14. Have you previously had a spiritual abortion(s)? ❑ Yes ❑No

15. What caused your spiritual abortion?

    ❑ Spiritual Ignorance   ❑Spiritual Bleeding   ❑Spiritual Torment

16. What infection signs can you identify that is causing your spiritual abortion

    _____   _____   _____
    _____   _____   _____
    _____   _____   _____

Prenatal Aftercare Treatment

Provide your patient with medical advice after care that would assist them from having a spiritual abortion.

_____
_____
_____
_____
_____
_____

Prescription Scripture (s)

_____
_____
_____
_____
_____
_____

Reflections:

_____
_____
_____
_____
_____
_____
_____
_____
_____
_____
_____
_____
_____
_____
_____
_____
_____
_____

Partial List of

Immunizations,

Infections, Disease,

& Allergies

Immunizations

1. Acceptance
2. Adoption
3. Affluence
4. Accessible
5. Appreciative
6. Authenticity
7. Balanced
8. Benevolent
9. Blameless
10. Boldness
11. Brilliant
12. Caring
13. Commitment
14. Compassion
15. Confidence
16. Consecration
17. Conscientiousness
18. Considerate
19. Conviction
20. Constant
21. Contemplative
22. Cooperative
23. Courage
24. Courteous
25. Creative
26. Dedicated
27. Deliverance
28. Dignified
29. Dependable
30. Determine
31. Devoted
32. Discernment
33. Discipleship
34. Discipline
35. Earnest
36. Edification
37. Efficient
38. Eloquent
39. Empathetic
40. Encouragement
41. Endurance
42. Enlightenment
43. Enthusiastic
44. Equipping
45. Eternal Life
46. Ethics
47. Evangelism
48. Fairness
49. Faith
50. Faithful
51. Firm
52. Flexible
53. Focused
54. Forbearance
55. Forgiving
56. Freedom
57. Friendly
58. Fruitfulness
59. Generosity
60. Gentleness
61. Genuine
62. Giving
63. Glorifying God
64. Goals
65. Goodness
66. Good Works
67. Gracious
68. Growth
69. Hardworking
70. Healthy
71. Helpful
72. Holiness
73. Honesty
74. Honor
75. Hopeful
76. Hospitality
77. Humility
78. Imaginative
79. Incorruptible
80. Independent
81. Innocence
82. Innovative
83. Inoffensive
84. Insightful
85. Insight
86. Integrity
87. Intelligent
88. Joy
89. Justification
90. Kindness
91. Knowledgeable
92. Leader
93. Love
94. Loyalty
95. Mature
96. Meekness
97. Mercifulness
98. Mercy
99. Moderate
100. Modesty
101. Morality
102. Nurturing

103. Obedience
104. Objective
105. Observant
106. Open
107. Optimistic
108. Orderly
109. Organized
110. Passionate
111. Patience
112. Peace
113. Perfection
114. Perseverance
115. Politeness
116. Praise
117. Predestination
118. Prosperity
119. Principled
120. Priorities
121. Privileges
122. Progress
123. Protective
124. Prudent
125. Punctual
126. Purposeful
127. Purity
128. Quietness
129. Coachable
130. Readiness
131. Receptive

132. Reconciliation
133. Reformation
134. Regeneration
135. Reliable
136. Resourceful
137. Repentance
138. Respect
139. Responsible
140. Responsive
141. Restoration
142. Reverence
143. Righteous
144. Salvation
145. Sanctification
146. Secure
147. Selfless
148. Self-Control
149. Self-Denial
150. Self-Discipline
151. Self-Examination
152. Self-Respect
153. Self-Sacrifice
154. Serious
155. Servanthood
156. Sharing
157. Silence
158. Skillful
159. Sociable
160. Sophisticated

161. Spiritual Growth
162. Spiritual Warfare
163. Stable
164. Steadfast
165. Strong
166. Studious
167. Sympathetic
168. Tasteful
169. Teachable
170. Testing
171. Thankful
172. Thorough
173. Tithing
174. Tolerant
175. Trusting
176. Trustworthy
177. Truthful
178. Understanding
179. Upright
180. Watchful
181. Weakness
182. Wisdom
183. Wise
184. Witnessing
185. Worthiness
186. Zeal

Infections/Diseases/ Allergies

1. Abomination
2. Abortions
3. Addiction
4. Adultery
5. Alienation
6. Anti-Christ
7. Arrogance
8. Astrology
9. Eviction
10. Barrenness
11. Bitterness
12. Blame
13. Blemish
14. Boasters
15. Boasting
16. Condemnation
17. Conformity
18. Corruption
19. Covenant Breakers
20. Coveting
21. Covetousness
22. Debauchery
23. Decay
24. Deceit
25. Dedication
26. Denial
27. Discord
28. Discouragement
29. Dishonesty
30. Disobedience
31. Disobedient
32. Disorder
33. Distrust
34. Division
35. Double-Mindedness
36. Doubt
37. Drunkenness
38. Dysfunctions
39. Envy
40. Evil
41. Factions
42. Failure
43. Faithless
44. False Gods
45. Falsehood
46. False Religion
47. False Teachers
48. False Teachings
49. False Witness
50. False Worship
51. Faults
52. Favoritism
53. Fear
54. Filthy Language
55. Fits Of Rage
56. Folly
57. Fools
58. Forgetting
59. Fornication
60. Godlessness
61. Godliness
62. Gossip
63. Grudge
64. Guilt
65. Hardness Of Heart
66. Hatred
67. Heresies
68. Homosexuality
69. Hopeless
70. Hypocrisy
71. Idolatry
72. Ignorance
73. Imagination
74. Imitating
75. Immorality
76. Impenitence
77. Imperfection
78. Impurity
79. Imputation
80. Insecurities
81. Intolerance
82. Low Self Esteem
83. Lack Of Confident
84. Jealousy
85. Legalism
86. Lewdness
87. Lies
88. Loneliness
89. Lust
90. Malice
91. Materialism
92. Mockery
93. Embarrassed
94. Murder
95. Neglect
96. Offence
97. Opposition
98. Oppression
99. Orgies
100. Pagans
101. Persecution
102. Poverty

103. Prejudice
104. Pride
105. Profanity
106. Quarreling
107. Rebellion
108. Regret
109. Rejection
110. Religion
111. Renunciation
112. Reputation
113. Riches
114. Ridicule
115. Scoffing
116. Self-Confidence
117. Self-Indulgence
118. Selfish Ambition
119. Selfishness

120. Self-Justification
121. Self-Righteousness
122. Sexual Immorality
123. Sexual Sin
124. Sickness
125. Sin-Bearer
126. Slander
127. Spite
128. Strife
129. Stubbornness
130. Substitution
131. Superstition
132. Suspicion
133. Temptation
134. Threats
135. Unbelief
136. Unbelievers

137. Uncircumcised
138. Undiscerning
139. Unfaithfulness
140. Unforgiveness
141. Unfruitfulness
142. Ungodliness
143. Unmerciful
144. Unrighteousness
145. Unselfishness
146. Untrustworthy
147. Urgency
148. Violent
149. Vulgarity
150. Whoremongles
151. Witchcraft
152. Worldliness
153. Worry

AUTHOR INFORMATION

Authors Bio

Kingdom Strategist, Blueprint Builder, and Spiritual Midwife **Pastor Derashay Zorn** is an international mentor and expert on the art of **unleashing purpose, developing dreams, and expanding untapped potentials within individuals, corporations, and ministries**. Her passion for information technology led her to obtain a Master of Science in Information System Management, which equipped her to specialize in analyzing, developing, and managing systems to birth or expand individuals and entities into the next dimension of kingdom implementation.

Mrs. Zorn has been an intricate part of community collaborations through bridging the gap between community entities. Derashay believes in building stronger communities through encouraging, empowering, and educating families. Mrs. Zorn has held various leadership positions within the community and has done extensive work in nonprofit organizations. Derashay has been involved in, but not limited to, nonprofit startups, technology analysis and implementation, online education platform design, implementation, and development, as well as establishing curriculums and training programs. In addition to being a wife and mother of three amazing sons, she is a pastor, entrepreneur, consultant, empowerment speaker, mentor, and friend.

As an overcomer of a chaotic life to an extraordinary life, Pastor Derashay has been given firsthand experience on how a life of principles can rearrange and position one's life to fulfill purpose. Her ability to overcome through the application of God's word has been the birthing grounds for Divine Order Restoration Ministries (D.O.R.M.) International where God has mandated her to "Restore the Order of God One Life, One Body, and One Nation at a Time." For such a time as this God has sent her forth to release Kingdom Strategies that will empower, educate, equip, and employ individuals into great dimension within their destinies.

Pastor Derashay equips mankind globally as the founder and host of the weekly "**In The Church**" **TV/Radio Broadcast** where they are shining the light of God's word "In the Church" to discuss and resolve real everyday issues that are taking place around the world exposes the good, the bad and the ugly. Mrs. Zorn's heart for women led her to equip them globally through her FREE digital *Women of Influence Magazine publication*. Under her leadership, she has implemented several educational biblical platforms to develop individuals daily within their purpose and prayer initiatives, such as the 365/24/7 International Prayer Call Center to motivate and encourage God's people.

Now, through **Kingdom Strategies University®** and her **School of Vision Bootcamp**, she teaches others **how to maximize their potential and monetize their gifts and talents** as a critical vehicle of fulfilling purpose, making significant impacts, and branding influence that can instantly and beautifully change the world.

Her philosophy is **"A critical tool to self-development is learning how to cultivate, build and release others into their destinies.**

Contact information

Email Address:

dzorn@divine-order.org

dzorn@inthechurch.com

dz@derashayzorn.com

Website:

Ministry	Business
www.divine-order.org	www.derashayzorn.com
www.inthechurch.com	

Social media:

Ministry	Business
Twitter: inthechurchlive	kbstrategist
Facebook: inthechurch	kingdombusinessstrategist
Instagram: inthechurch	kingdomstrategist

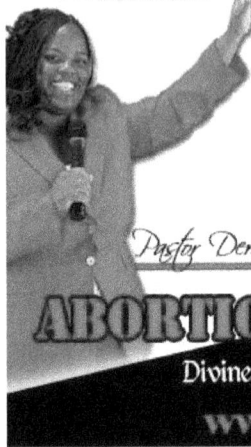

NO MORE ABORTIONS CAMPAIGN

JOIN THE CAMPAIGN

✔ MAKE THE PLEDGE
✔ PURCHASE THE BOOK
✔ BOOK ME
✔ HOST A CAMPAIGN EVENT
   (RETREAT, CONFERENCE, SUMMIT, ETC)

✔ SPONSOR A CAMPAIGN EVENT
✔ JOIN IN A CAMPAIGN EVENT
✔ SHARE THE CAMPAIGN

Pastor Derashay Zorn

ABORTIONS IN THE CHURCH
Divine Strategies to Spiritual Deliverance
www.inthechurch.com

Make The Pledge: Make the pledge to give birth to your purpose, dreams, visions, goals, desires, etc. Obtain your Delivering Greatness commitment seal. Join the Birthing Chambers FB group and be a part of a nurturing environment/community for giving birth and expanding in your purpose. Go to www.inthechurch.com

Purchase The Book: Obtain a few copies of the book and be a blessing to a few people. Go to www.inthechurch.com

Book Me: Book me as your keynote speaker, workshop facilitator, motivational speaker, intercessor at your next event. Go to www.derashayzorn.com

Host a Campaign Event (retreat, conference, seminar, summit, etc): Host an event that is centered around birthing out purpose, dreams, visions, goals, etc. and include us in the party

Join a Campaign Event: Watch out for our upcoming local, state, national or international events, register and get engaged in the movement. Watch out for the Summer & Winter Conference, Fall Birthing Chambers Retreat, and a host of webinars.

Sponsor a Campaign Event: Become a sponsor by taking part in events sponsorship opportunities.

Share The Campaign: Share the campaign information with others you know that could benefit from joining the movement

Conference / Summit/Seminar/Speaking Empowerment Topics and Training

I'm Pregnant with Possibilities

Delivering my Expectations

Planned Pregnancy

I Think I'm pregnant

Overcoming/Avoiding the Pitfalls of having a spiritual miscarriage, abortion & stillborn

Avoiding SIDS

False Labor Pain

Avoiding Premature Birth

Resuscitate my baby

Balancing my pregnancy

How to deliver a healthy baby

Trusting others with you baby

My baby need to grow up

It takes a village to raise this baby

My Baby Just L.E.A.P

Kingdom Business: Non-Negotiable

B.O.S.S. (Birthing Out Successful Solutions) Business Strategy Series

F Factors (Fear. Faith. Favor)

Customized programs or topics upon request

Look out for other titles

The Birthing Process

Spiritual Midwife Training Manual

Preserving Destiny through the Power of Prayer: A Spiritual Warfare Prayer Collection

Rules of Success: Investment 101

Called from the Grave – The Resurrection

.

www.ingramcontent.com/pod-product-compliance
Lightning Source LLC
Chambersburg PA
CBHW062044090426
42740CB00016B/3020